MORE THAN

The 4 Missing Pieces Needed To Become Who You Were Meant To Be

By Laura-Jane Hand

To Hanna,
Enjoy learning about
the 4 missing pieces!

Love
Laura-Jane
xxx.

Email: **laurajanehand8@gmail.com**
Website: **www.laurajanehand.com**
Instagram: **@laurajanehand**
Linked In: **linkedin.com/in/laurajanehand**
Podcast link: **wavve.link/laurajanehand**

DEDICATED TO:

YOU. Because you know you're capable of more.

CONTENTS

Introduction
Before We Begin

Part 1: The Theory

MISSING PIECE NO 1: Your BODY
THE NOT-SO MISSING PIECE: Your MIND (But DEEPER)
MISSING PIECE NO 2: Your HEART
MISSING PIECE NO 3: Your SPIRIT
MISSING PIECE NO 4: Your SOUL

Part 2: The Experience

The 'Experience' Introduction
The DAILY Experience

Final Thoughts

INTRODUCTION

I'm so glad you're here.

If you're anything like me, you've spent years sensing that you're capable of more. You've seen glimpses of the person you were created to be and the potential lying dormant within you. It's a version of yourself you've craved to know. A happier and stronger version where you feel fearless, powerful and content. It's a state you've experienced momentarily but feels out of reach consistently because it almost seems too good to be true. It's like there's a battle going on within your mind where you're aware of two lives - the one you're living and the one you want to live. You know you have the capability, the desire and the dream, but you don't move. It's like you're psychologically paralysed.

Albeit subtle at times and often unrecognised, you move through life with your head down, and with a general feeling of smallness and unworthiness. You find yourself holding back, never fully expressing all that you're truly capable of and it prevents you from stepping onto the front row of your life. After spending years seeking approval from everyone and everything outside of yourself, you still haven't found what you believe you're missing. You've mastered the art of self-destruction and it seems like all you can manifest is chaos and drama. At times you self-sabotage your good. At times you don't even know what you want. Nothing ever seems good enough and that includes yourself.

You've tried to raise your vibe. You've tried to attract what you want. You've written goals and read an entire library of self-help books, but even though you've been affirming you're good enough, deserving and successful, you still don't actually feel it. Although you've experienced mini breakthroughs and 'Aha!' moments along the way, you still haven't received the permanent solution you'd hoped for. You're exhausted with trying to improve yourself. You're tired of holding back. You're fed up of feeling inadequate and low.

Yet the part of you which knows you have the ability to be happier and a more powerful force in the world is nudging you more and more each day. Instead of wondering if your life will ever take off; instead of working against the person you see every day in the mirror and instead of constantly looking outside of yourself to find what you think you're missing, buying into thoughts of smallness, fear and self-doubt which seem to scream at you all day long. The tiring, endless pursuit to overcome it all can stop. You're ready for the actual answer now. The solution that's always been closer than you'd imagined.

The problem is though, we've been taught the opposite. We're brainwashed into believing the next product, person or place will solve everything. We grow up believing we're missing something, yet no-one seems to know exactly what that is. We give away our power by comparing ourselves endlessly with other people. We've bought into our sense of inadequacy and placed so much attention on overcoming it that all we've managed to do is create more of the same.

Wherever we look we're told that our mindset is the key, the answer to all of our problems. Yet no matter how much mindset work we do, we just can't seem to get out of our own way. If anything, our mind seems to be constantly working against us and it's a story we can live on repeat for years. This sense of confusion and depression can seem to be too deep and too painful to be able to overcome by just repeating an affirmation, tapping our way out of, or creating another list of SMART goals we quickly lose passion for.

As the former Queen of Inadequacy and Self-Doubt, I always felt like something was stopping me and holding me back from being myself. I kept reading it was all about love, but I struggled with either feeling it towards myself or giving it to others without fear of being screwed over again. So I built walls around my heart to protect me from experiencing any more pain. Something in my past didn't go as I'd planned,

2

someone didn't treat me the way I'd expected them too and somehow along the way, I'd learned to close my heart. I thought these walls would protect me from others, but all they did was cause me more pain. I went out searching for answers hoping the world would solve all of my problems and soothe my pain. And every time I was left disappointed.

After years of trial and error, seeking out the best spiritual gurus, spending a fortune on therapies, therapists, teachers, mentors and courses, reading and dissecting the most complex spiritual texts, travelling the world to find the answer, to find the secret to overcoming the blockages within me: the answer arrived. Not when I was at a super-spiritual yoga retreat OM'ing all night and day or in bright flashing lights on a New York Times Square newsreel. It came in one of those life defining moments you never forget. One of those moments of awakening you read about people experiencing, but somehow believe they're only available to the spiritual elite in some over dramatic or elaborate way.

As I packed my bags in search of yet another guru who would solve all of my problems, leaving home for a month to go and find myself again, that moment hit me like lightening. There wasn't a big fanfare or sudden appearance of an army of angels, but as I sat in my seat waiting for the plane to take off for another month of soul-searching, at the exact moment the doors closed, it was like a switch went off inside my head. I burst into tears. I'd had a sudden realisation. I knew the answer.

If you've watched Friends, the one where Rachel was leaving Ross to go and live in Paris, and she's on the plane waiting for it to take off, you know what's coming next. "I need to get off the plane", I cried to the bemused cabin crew who were trying to calm me down whilst the rest of the passengers tried to discreetly see what was going on. However, unlike Rachel, I couldn't get off the plane. The doors were locked and the plane started to move. But what happened on that long, lonely flight made me realise with crystal clear clarity what I needed to do next.

With every self-help book I'd read, there was a point I just wasn't getting. Each book or course would take me so far, but then I'd revert to the same old habits and operating system. When I was fed up of feeling the same way and experiencing the same results, despite the amount of self-development and mindset work I was doing, I now knew what was really going on. The penny had finally dropped.

And this is the moment **More Than A Mindset** was born.

Despite all of the focus on improving our mindset, why are so many people still so depressed, down and suicidal? Why are so many people meandering through life not reaching their potential? Why are so many people suffering so much and not reaching the levels of success they deserve? We've been doing the positive thinking, the meditating and the affirmations, but they don't appear to be as transformative as we're told they should be. We've been trying to manifest what we want, but there seems to always be a block in our way. Clearly there's something missing. Clearly the mindset work isn't enough.

If we only work on our mindset alone, it keeps us trapped because we're focusing on changing something we don't like inside of our minds: our thought patterns, our beliefs and our outlook. And we're trapped because we're not getting to the root cause. If we only work on our mindsets, we're not going deep enough because that's not where our pain lies. Our barriers live somewhere else. By only focusing on our mindset, we're not working on the 4 other aspects of our psyche which are often overlooked. These 4 other areas have a huge impact upon on our mindset; it could even be argued that they shape our mindset. Yet if they're not worked on in totality, then it's no wonder we remain disconnected and unsure of ourselves, despite the amount of mindset work we do.

The hurt we've experienced in the past is intellectually held onto within our minds, it's where we try to make sense of it all and whilst uplifting our thought patterns will help us, that's not where we're healed because the pain we carry is in our hearts. The anger and resentment we hold onto from experiences in the past and the patterns of inadequacy and fear we've learned in our childhood, makes us build walls around our hearts to protect us from ever experiencing any pain again. Instead of protecting us, all this does is affect what we choose to then think, perceive and believe within our minds. Our spirit a.k.a our attitude is then impacted because we're in a constant state of attack and defence, always protecting ourselves from potential lovelessness from other people, and ready to attack back at a moments notice.

Our body and all of its functions are knocked out of balance because of the turmoil that's going on inside of us. We're not at peace inside of ourselves and this internal dis-ease causes us numerous undesirable symptoms. The messages from our soul which is always nudging us to grow, can't get through this internal chaos so we feel even more lost and alone. And in the moments where we do get a sense or a message from our Higher Self, we write it off because it almost seems too good to be true. This whirlwind of crazy energy we live in is only creating more of the same because we're not going deep enough. We're not experiencing the true transformative power of the mindset work we're doing so we're always left searching. Yet the answer lies right inside of us, closer than we've ever realised.

It took me years of searching and heartache to realise the mindset work was only going to get me so far, and it was only when I started to go deeper that things really began to change. Going deep into our hearts is a place we've been unknowingly avoiding for a long time. Maybe opening it up again would make us remember some of the pain. Maybe going there it would remind us of everything we've been missing out on. But the real reason we avoid going there is because we somehow know that if we did, that's the place where our life would be amazing and everything would start to work. So we subconsciously resist it and self-sabotage any good which comes our way. This is where we're trying to protect ourselves from ever being hurt again, but all this does is stop us from experiencing everything we've been searching for and more.

And this is why the work we need to do is more than just working on our mindset, because our mind actually gets in our way and stops us from going deep enough. What I learned on that flight made me realise that we don't need a trip to the Himalayas to meditate for a month to help sort us out. We can do it in our own front room, or in any room, in any moment. Running away hoping someone or something else would solve everything was just another avoidance tactic. Waiting for another solution is just another delay thought up by our clever mind to always keep us seeking love but never actually experiencing it. And we can go there in any moment, once we can move past our mind.

As cheesy as it sounds, when we do allow ourselves to go to the love within our hearts instead of avoiding it, it feels like we're coming home. It's where we start to feel like ourselves again. It's where everything starts to make sense again. It's where depression lifts, inadequacy fades away and our life begins to work like we've always sensed it could. It's where all of our strength and power lies.

So what's the answer?

All we need to do is let ourselves go there more consistently.

Since you've stayed with me this far, I'm assuming you'll know this sounds easier said than done, right? Loving ourselves and others without holding back, and believing and backing ourselves seems harder than coming up with this weeks winning lottery numbers.

So the next question is: **how?**

This book is split into the 5 areas we need to work on and I've made it super-clear how we go deeper, past our mind that actively resists everything good. So we'll go through:

1. What theses 5 areas are

2. Why they're blocked and

3. How we access them.

Accessing our inner strength and becoming the person we know deep down we know we can be doesn't need to be such a complex, life sucking, energy draining, time consuming process. When we work on all 5 areas, the whole process begins to fall in to place.

So **More Than A Mindset** enables us to:

1. Re-set our nervous system by taking us out of the constant fight or flight mode we've been dwelling in. This means we're able to let go of the stress and strain and the fear and the anxiety we've been feeling, so we can start to think and see clearly again. Once we start to let go of all of the weight we carry on our shoulders and we finally give ourselves permission to let go, it's amazing how quickly the Universe responds. This is where we enter a flow state, where life works in ways we could never plan ourselves.

2. We'll go deeper inside our minds than we've ever accessed before, going beyond our intellectual mind, beyond the reasoning, the fear, the noise and the distractions to the

place where we can find all of the answers, clarity and peace we've been searching for.

3. We'll break through the walls we've built around our hearts so we can start to experience the love we have within ourselves again. This is the place where our hearts can triple in size. If you've ever watched The Grinch, you'll know what I mean. This is where we start to become ourselves again, no more holding back or fearing what may or may not happen. This is where we find our inner strength.

However, this is the point where that sneaky little voice inside our heads begins to doubt what we're reading and questioning if all of this is just "too good to be true." So we're going to face those doubts head on:

Yeh but…

Is this really achievable? Is this just another self-help book that'll feel good at the time but then be forgotten about in a few days, or even in a few hours time?

More Than A Mindset is exactly what it says it is. It means we'll create changes inside of ourselves which go deeper than we normally access when we just focus on working on our mindset. We go past the mind, which can get in the way of us going deeper, to make the changes we know we want to experience but we just can't seem to get there.

Yeh but…

I don't have time to fit in any daily habits because life is so busy, work is so hectic and the school run eats up my entire life!!

That's why we're focusing on all 5 areas in one go, going deeper and making more of a profound change within us. It doesn't mean to say it takes any longer, it's about switching on the right parts of us by going straight to the place where the most powerful change happens. It's like electricity, always waiting to light up the room when we just switch on the light. And the more we do this, the quicker and easier it becomes.

Yeh but…

I've tried to sort this out before and it's not worked, so why will it work this time?

It took me years to learn what the missing pieces were, and not only that, how to actually apply them. I hope this book helps you to not waste one more day dragging yourself through the day, hoping things will work out, feeling anxious, afraid of what may or may not happen, comparing yourself, holding yourself back, beating yourself down and waiting for your life to take off whilst continuing to wonder why it hasn't yet.

When the searching for another solution stops, when we stop numbing ourselves, avoiding ourselves, maxing out our credit cards and endlessly scrolling and comparing ourselves on social media. When we refuse to play it small for one more minute, that's when things begin to change. When we begin to take our power back, the confusion and self-doubt begins to disappear and we finally take on the role of master of our own destiny. Instead of being controlled and consumed by a never ending influx of fear from within and without, we start to own every aspect of our personality and begin to get out of our own way.

If you've read all of the books, signed up to all of the courses, meditated, gotten yourself into some crazy yoga positions, drank the green juices, created vision boards and said affirmations to change your life. If you've tried to believe in yourself and love yourself and something still hasn't clicked. Then all you need to know is that it's all totally possible and it doesn't need to take so long.

This book will help you to overcome the lower aspect of your personality and that little voice that seems to scream at you all day long, and instead finally turn on your Higher Self - the person you know you can be. It sounds cheesy and overused, and possibly even over promised and under delivered. Once we do this properly, everything starts to fall in to place. We just need to make the first move and we'll be helped more than we can imagine. When we work on more than our mindset alone, we begin to experience profound change from the inside-out and our life will never be the same again.

Are you ready to become the person you were meant to be…?

Let's do this.
Love,

Laura-Jane x

BEFORE WE BEGIN

SO WHAT IS...
'MORE THAN A MINDSET'?

More Than A Mindset was created out of frustration. Frustration that through all of the advice telling us 'Mindset is the KEY', through all of the self-help books on the subject, the millions of affirmations and work we can do on our minds, why are so many people still so depressed, down and suicidal? Why are so many people meandering through life not reaching their potential? Why are so many people suffering so much and living in fear?

Surely something is missing.

Did you know that 95% of our mental activity occurs at a subconscious level, which means it happens automatically without our control? Our conscious mind - the mind we operate from day to day - represents only 5% of our thoughts and is the part of our brain which sees lack and limitation everywhere and impresses our subconscious mind with what it sees. So, if you think about it, that means when we're working on positive thinking we're only using 5% of our brain's capacity and it's the same part of our brain that will instinctively challenge what we're positively affirming, because it's so different from what we currently believe.

So, when we're affirming: "I am enough, I am love, I am <fill in the blank>", our conscious mind will subtly question us, and it's so subtle it almost goes unheard, until we gradually 'forget' our affirmations and stop practising them. This in turn proves to our ego that we're powerless and nothing ever changes. Of course, some of our efforts will penetrate to our subconscious mind, but the work we're putting in completely misses out other essential factors which make up our entire being, such as all the ways we subconsciously block our good.

Underneath our conscious mind lies an entire network of beliefs, fears, behaviours, thoughts, feelings and emotions. For example, if our heart has been bruised, we'll shut down, and until we've healed this aspect of our personality, then affirming: "I am love" will make little impact. At that point we tend to turn to another book, attend another course, write new goals and say new affirmations and we set off with the right intentions, but in reality we don't actually see any real progress because we're not healing the *source* of the problem. We're not going deep enough.

LET'S GO DEEPER

The superconscious mind is the mind we access when we alter our consciousness through practices like breathing and meditation. It's the divine, creative mind of infinite intelligence and wisdom. It's the space where we can hear our own internal guidance and where we come to realise how amazing we actually are. By going deeper, higher and further than we've ever gone before, our souls are freed, our spirits are uplifted, our hearts are healed, and our minds are transformed. It's the combination of accessing all aspects of our psyche which is where the real transformation lies. And it's in the consistent application of certain practices which enables us to experience the thoughts, feelings and emotions, the connection, the flow and the alignment that we've been seeking.

* Going *deeper* means we're accessing all the power, potential and love that's within us, that's currently just covered up.

* Going *higher* means we're willing to embrace our Higher Self - the person we know we can be.

* Going *further* means we're willing to overcome the limits that have been holding us back.

The purpose of this book isn't to learn another set of practices and not apply them, but to actually begin to use them daily so we can change from the inside-out. **Part 1** of the book is called: **The Theory**, where we'll go through the mindset work but also the 4 other missing pieces.

There's nothing new in this book, and I certainly can't take credit for any of the practices we look at. Weirdly we've been taught about each of them for thousands of years, just in ways we didn't always resonate with. But what I have done is spent years applying them, adapting them, figuring out what works and what doesn't and interpreting them for our modern busy life.

Part 2 of the book is called: **The Experience.** This is where we'll go through all of the exercises we can do which allow us to experience the person we were meant to be on a daily basis.

Are you ready to know the 4 other areas...?

PART 1:
THE THEORY

MISSING PIECE NO 1
YOUR **BODY**

***

Corporate world always felt strange to me. Everyone always seemed stressed, under pressure and couldn't wait for the weekend. Monday mornings were often approached slowly and sluggishly and suddenly everyone began to come alive on Fridays. Before I had the confidence to leave that world, I'd gone down the path of Banking for many years because quite frankly, the pay was great, more than any other industry for my line of work. It felt pretty soulless to be honest and although I tried to be grateful for the work, I just couldn't seem to fall in love with it. I always knew there was something 'out there' more rewarding I should be doing with my life, but I was afraid and far too confused to be able to make any significant progress to creating a decent and clear exit plan.

One of the girls I sat next to kept complaining about headaches and having the odd day off here and there because of them. She'd sit with her head in her hands before, during and after conference calls - which was pretty much all day long. As we sat next to each other, she began to open up about issues she was facing and how she was feeling at times. She was a smart girl and very good at her job but when I asked her a perfectly normal question regarding her headaches and how I might know a way to help get rid of them without drugs, she shot me down. Ok, so my approach might have seemed different, but on the other hand, it wasn't because we've all done it since the moment we were created inside our mothers' wombs. It's something we do all day, everyday… so you'd think we'd be a master at it. But we're not. In fact, we're surprisingly shocking at it.

When she came into the office again complaining of another headache, I asked her a question I quickly regretted. She was clearly struggling and although her issue appeared as headaches, other people experience digestive issues, menstrual problems, burn out, sleep issues, lack of sex drive and a number of other undesirable symptoms. So I jumped in with both feet and asked her, "Are you breathing correctly?" She snapped back, "Of course I'm breathing correctly - I'm alive aren't I?" And I said, "Well yes, you're alive, but you're not thriving, because you've just told me that your life isn't working on a number of levels and a practice as simple as focusing on your breath could start to change all that." Which is completely true, but she just thought I was mad.

***

Have you ever considered how you're breathing?

Likewise, have you ever noticed times when you're *not* breathing?

Our breath is a key indicator as to what's going on within our minds. If we're stressed and anxious, or happy and peaceful, then our state of mind will be reflected in the quality of our breathing. At times, we're not even breathing at all. At the moment, the only proven way of shifting us away from a stress state into a more peaceful state isn't something we can go out and buy, neither is it found by repeating an affirmation. It's to do with the quality of our breathing. Watching a baby breathing provides us with a perfect example of how to breathe optimally. Babies and young children breathe deeply and rhythmically into their naturally relaxed bellies. As they're so free of tension, their bellies expand fully and relax gracefully. Their exhale is naturally longer than their inhale, and their chests remain relatively still.

THE PROBLEM:
WHY WE STRUGGLE TO BREATHE

This unhindered way of breathing changed at some point in our childhood when we became frightened or distressed. Maybe we experienced some emotional or physical violence, shock, pain or trauma, and as a result we automatically began to shallow breathe into our chests instead of breathing into our bellies. This created a psychological habit that we repeated each time we faced a stressful situation.

Our inability to breathe well is also due to various social and cultural factors which mean that most of us now habitually breathe into our chests in a shallow and rapid way. The stresses and pressure of modern life, along with our perceived sense of urgency and inadequacy, is reflected in our breathing. We've also lost the art of relaxation and we're unable to fully let go, which is reflected in our inability to exhale. Our default mode to take more on, do more and have more is taking its toll and is showing in our rapid inhale and our non-existent exhales.

The tension we unknowingly hold around our stomach and chest prevents the freedom of movement we require to breathe optimally. When we breathe deeply into our diaphragm, allowing our belly to relax and expand, and we allow the exhale to be released slowly and gently, we're telling our body that we're relaxed. Our long exhale is an indication to every cell in our body that we're safe.

THE STRESS ZONE

Most of the time we live in a constant state of 'fight or flight'. It has become natural for us to live at this speed and intensity. We've been told to go out there and make things happen, to pursue our dreams and never give up. We're bombarded with an ever-increasing array of things we can buy and things we can achieve. We hold on to the steering wheel of our lives so tightly, it's like we're in the world's fastest racing car. The tension in our necks and shoulders has become normal. Our jaws don't know what it feels like to be relaxed.

We're told we can manifest anything we want to by this date and in this exact way, but we don't consider if it's what we really want or whether we're just going along with what society tells us we should be doing. What if the things we're asking for aren't for our highest good? What if we're asking too small? We can't see it yet because we look out into the world through our limited vision. We're a marketer's dream because we're consuming more than ever, and we're a government's dream because we need to keep earning in order to fund our excessive lifestyles and to pay for those endless products we don't really need. We're so used to setting goals and striving for things and we feel like failures if our desires don't manifest in line with our timescales, or other people's.

We're asked to let go and to trust, but we panic because we don't know how to do that. If anything we feel like we should really be getting more done - have you seen the size of our to-do lists? Have you seen what we think we need to achieve just to gain a microscopic amount of external approval and success? Our nervous systems are firing adrenaline around our bodies with the intention of protecting us, but it's knocking us completely out of balance. Our bodies are nudging us to tell us we're off track and then we're sold a cure to fix it. These cures promise us we'll be pretty enough, good enough, more successful, healthier and healed if we just buy this one more item which we don't really need, but in reality - it's just one more distraction from the Truth.

OUR NERVOUS SYSTEM

The largest nerve in our body runs adjacent to our throats and controls every system and function inside of us. It's called the vagus nerve and it's controlled by our breath because of where it's located. If we're in the stress zone then that nerve is being run by adrenaline and cortisol, and the emotions of stress and fear are in charge. That means we're not breathing effectively, and over time this has a detrimental impact on our body's health. If fear and stress are running the show, then it's likely we're making decisions based on these two emotions too.

What we perceive in the world begins with what's going on inside us. For example, if we think this is an unfriendly, limited Universe, then this becomes our experience in life. It's a cycle, but it's one we can manipulate and change through the conscious act of breathing optimally. If we're breathing correctly, we can control the functioning of this nerve, the quality of our breath, and its impact on the functioning of our entire body. This changes everything, because we're taken out of 'fight or flight' mode.

FIGHT OR FLIGHT MODE	RELAXED MODE
STRESS ZONE	PEACE ZONE
STRESS HORMONE	BALANCED HORMONES
CONSTIPATION	GREAT ELIMINATION
FIGHT OR FLIGHT / ADRENALINE	MORE RELAXED / HAPPY HORMONES
FUEL IS GLUCOSE	FUEL IS FAT
NO GOD / NO LOVE / NO TRUST	GOD / LOVE / TRUST
CONTROL	LET GO

THE IMPACT OF STRESS ON OUR BODY

The stress zone is when we're in a fight mode. In the past, our stress came from threats to our survival from danger, famine and war, so when we're in this stress state now, the adrenaline and cortisol released into our bodies gives us the energy to run from the sorts of extreme physical threats we're no longer exposed to in modern life. Our blood supply is diverted into our arms and our legs so we can run from danger and that has a knock-on impact on other non-essential parts of our body such as our hair, nails and fertility.

When our levels of adrenaline and cortisol are high, our body thinks we're in danger and we're going to starve, so it instinctively begins to protect us by slowing down the production of progesterone. This causes havoc with our fertility because the last thing our body wants to do is to bring a new baby into this kind of stressful environment. Progesterone acts as a natural anti-depressant but because it's slowed down, not only are we stressed, but the natural cure our body makes to heal us and uplift our mood is slowed down. Our state of mind is then affected, so we're more inclined to become anxious, fearful and depressed, and our entire natural physical and non-physical balance becomes disrupted.

Our digestion slows down too because less energy is being sent there, which causes numerous undesirable symptoms. It also means we're holding on to excess waste that we don't need, which doesn't make us feel good either. Not only do we lose the production of a hormone that helps us to digest our food and take in nutrients, but stress makes us rush through our food without even chewing it properly which has a detrimental effect on our digestion. We haven't got time to sit down and enjoy a meal in peace, so we're quickly shovelling down a sandwich as we type. If we're not focused on the task of eating mindfully, then we're not going to benefit fully from our organic healthy food and fancy supplements.

Because we're stressed, we're more likely to be drinking caffeine, which has the same impact on our bodies as adrenaline and isn't conducive to a healthy, balanced body. Because we're stressed, our bodies want a quick hit of fuel, so we use our glucose stores first and then need to top them back up again fast, so our food choices suffer and we tend to crave more sugar.

So our body, in its glorious wisdom, thinks it's helping us by slowing down the production of progesterone. All because of stress. Which means that all the systems of our body are impacted too. We've lost the production of a hormone that naturally stops us from being depressed and anxious and the result is that we feel awful. Our mood is affected and the choices we make in our lives are impacted too. We're down, and we can potentially go down even further. We're offered anti-depressants to help us, but rather than healing the cause of our problem, they're just masking the pain. We're told to work on our mindset to change everything because "mindset is the key" but after time, we begin to wonder if there's more going on here.

A NEW KIND OF STRESS

We might not be running from famine and war, but we have lots of different stresses to contend with and our bodies are reacting in exactly the same way as they would have done thousands of years ago. Now we're stressed about our finances, relationships, businesses, careers and perceived levels of success. We feel like we're under constant pressure and everything needs to happen yesterday. We're in a state of perpetual 'not enough-ness' which is sending us into a constant stress mode of striving and grasping. As humans we can survive in that mode for short periods – in fact it can sometimes lead to heightened productivity and provide us with direction and motivation – but when we're living in that state constantly, that's where the problem lies.

When we're in the stress zone we're controlling, busy, distracted and unhappy, but we don't always know it because we're masking it with food, drink and other distractions which are keeping us trapped in the stress cycle. We're busy being busy. If we've chosen a heavy, sugary meal that evening and we've had to have a few drinks to chill out after work, then it's less likely we'll jump out of bed the next day to exercise or meditate. It's so normal to us we don't know of any other way to live and often we need a nudge to tell us we're in this state.

When we receive the nudge, in whatever form it comes to us, it's our body's way of giving us a message. For some it might appear as a skin rash, or for others it might appear as digestive issues, or fertility problems, but it's our body's way of asking us to review our entire lifestyle and think about what we eat, take, drink, think, say, do, feel, believe and perceive. It's asking us to work from the inside out. It's asking us to work on a level deeper than our mindset.

BODY: EXERCISE

How are you breathing now? Is there tension in your stomach? Are you actually breathing much at all? It helps to analyse your body - is there any tension in your head, between your eyebrows, behind your eyes, in your cheeks, in your jaw, in your neck, across your chest, around your heart, or in your stomach, hips, bottom, legs, knees or feet? Are you breathing into your chest or stomach? Are you holding your breath? Are you inhaling fully in to your belly? Are you actually exhaling at all? Do you feel energised or tired, calm or anxious, happy or sad? Let your breath be your guide.

Another way to check your breathing is to lie down on your back with one hand on your chest and one hand on your lower belly and just breathe. Notice which hand is moving. If your top hand is moving you're chest breathing, which means you're probably feeling stressed, low or anxious. If your bottom hand is moving you're belly breathing or breathing into your diaphragm, so you're probably feeling more centred and relaxed.

Chest breathing creates more stress in the body and our minds and therefore in our lives. We're in a cycle that continues to perpetuate until we decide to make a change. Our inhales can be constricted because it's not fashionable to walk around with a relaxed, loose Buddha belly, unlike a baby who doesn't care. Society tells us we should have a toned, flat belly, but this has detrimental effects on how deeply we can breathe, creating stress and tension around our upper abdomen and heart. Skinny jeans look great, but they're not helping us to breathe either.

THE BEST PART ABOUT BELLY BREATHING

Belly breathing is where our top hand remains quite still and our lower hand is the hand that's moving. Belly breathing can feel uncomfortable or even slightly painful at first due to the tension we've accumulated over the years. This tension is the stress, fear, grasping and controlling. And the best part about belly breathing is that it allows us to release unprocessed emotions that we're holding on to, without having to know or work out what they are. So instead of trying to intellectualise what's not right or working inside our minds - which can produce even more stress, we can relax knowing that as long as we're breathing deeply into our bellies, then everything we need to let go of will go. It allows us to remain fully in the present, away from any anxiety of the future, any regrets of the past or obsessing over any concerns we have in the present.

Even as I'm typing, I have to constantly remind myself to breathe, let alone breathe correctly. When we're immersed in a task, or we're stressed, anxious or working to a deadline, we can forget to breathe at all. Notice which situations tempt you into shallow chest breathing. Maybe it's when you're feeling nervous, stressed or inadequate. Maybe it's when you're at work and you're under pressure to complete a task, so your mind shuts down and becomes cloudy and you struggle to focus. If you were asked to take a break and to breathe deeply and rhythmically for a few minutes, you'd come back to the task from a new calmer perspective, and you'd feel like a completely different person.

I can hear my teacher saying: "It all starts with the breath." Yet it took me years to realise he had a point!

THE PEACE ZONE
LET'S RECONNECT

When our minds are consumed with uncertainty and disorder and we're controlling life ourselves, the manipulation of our breathing allows us to reconnect to our peace and power by taking us out of 'fight or flight' mode and bringing our awareness back into the body. 'Fight or flight' mode is activated by the stress and situations in our lives that cause us pain and it's an indication of our inability to let go, but we struggle to do that because we're not really sure what it means to let go or what we need to let go of. We also wonder if we do eventually let go, how will everything work out and who will sort everything out for us. We're told there's a power greater than us who will step forward and help us once we let go. But we've spent years not knowing what this power is and actively disowning its existence, and if we do recognise it, we don't always know how to access it. Not only that but we secretly worry that it's been so long since we've recognised it that it might have forgotten about us or completely deserted us all together.

THE SOLUTION

We think letting go means we don't care, which we equate with lack of achievement or progress, but actually we've been taught for thousands of years that in order for our lives to work, we need to let go. However this takes work, because we're not used to trusting that everything will work out for our highest good. *A Course In Miracles* says: **"You cannot conceive of all of the happiness that comes to you without your planning."** (W-p1.135.26:2) But this can't happen if we're trusting in our own strength alone. So who or what do we trust in?

The Bible teaches us: **"Be diligent to enter that rest"** (Hebrews 4:11.) which means it takes effort to learn to step back and trust and it takes effort to relax. Just to be clear, I'm no expert on the Bible but when I learned what the messages meant in a different way than how we're typically taught, *and* practised them, they started to make much more sense because they actually worked. So we have to be diligent, because it requires work on our part to reach this state of 'being' instead of a constant state of 'doing' and we have to be disciplined to make room in our lives for personal wellbeing. It's not selfish, because we'll actually be a better husband, wife, parent, colleague, employer and friend but it normally takes a nudge for us to remember to do it.

Because we're taught to fight more than we're taught to trust, it means we're actually blocking our good, because in this state there's no room for the Universe to help us. When we step back and make space for all of the world's strength and power to help us, we give it the opportunity to work on our behalf. We have to make the first move by stepping back, letting go and letting the Universe help us out. If the whole 'trusting in the Universe' feels weird and wacky, it's only because we've been so used to relying on our own strength alone.

***

TRUE HEALING

From this enlightened perspective we're able to experience our invulnerability and strength. We're healing ourselves on a level deeper than our psyche is used to, because our health is achieved through the proper perspective of our wholeness and our willingness to awaken to this knowledge. We experience healing when we overcome the fear of awakening to our Higher Self - the part of us which knows we can let go and that everything will be ok. Our wholeness is when we remember we're not alone here. The voice of our intelligence, our inner teacher gets louder the more willing we become to listen to it, but we can only do that once we've let go and allowed the power within us to override our attempts to control everything ourselves.

HOW TO LET GO

A couple of years ago, my husband and I were on a track day with an incredible man who trained Formula One drivers. We were driving a Porsche 911 around an open airfield at over 100mph and I was gripping the wheel so hard that my knuckles were white. I was hardly breathing and screaming all the way round. The instructor asked that on my next turn I should relax and trust that the car knew what it was doing. He asked me to move the steering wheel with only my left little finger and to keep my right hand on my leg. He wanted me to understand that the car didn't need my force and tight grip to turn the corner. It could move just as effectively with the lightest of touches. And it did. The car turned the corner perfectly at 120mph with just my left little finger moving the steering wheel. I was amazed.

And that's how life is.

We don't need to grip onto the imaginary steering wheel of our lives and be on a constant white knuckle ride. We can let go. We can step out of 'fight or flight' mode and relax. Believing we're being supported isn't a weakness. Believing we're more powerful than we appear to be isn't being arrogant or deluded - it's where we're beginning to understand who we really are and what we're capable of. And this is why the body work is the first part we need to focus on before we do all of the mind work because we're bringing ourselves down from the craziness of the world, back into our centres. We're coming out of fight or flight so we can start to think and see clearly again. We're preparing the way for the mind work we're doing to be as transformative as we're promised it can be.

HOW TO CHANGE ALL OF THIS

There are eight aspects of yoga but we're normally only aware of one or two: the physical moves and meditation. But there are also a number of breathing techniques called Pranayamas, which existed long before the yoga postures we've become familiar with. The name sounds fancy but Prana is just our breath, our life force. These breathing exercises are an undervalued aspect of yoga but they have the ability to create positive changes within us at a deep level because "It all starts with the breath." Pranayama teaches us how to breathe correctly and we begin by simply controlling our breathing through the conscious regulation of our inhale and exhale.

LET'S GET SLIGHTLY TECHNICAL FOR A MINUTE

Our autonomic nervous system manages processes in our bodies which we don't normally have control over, such as our digestion, elimination, the beating of our hearts and the movement of the lungs. Pranayama is connected directly to the autonomic nervous system, so it brings these functions under its control through deep, diaphragmatic breathing. This ensures all systems and functions are optimised, because essential oxygen is being sent to all the body's vital organs increasing their efficiency.

Most people have around 300 million alveoli on their lungs and if these could be flattened out, they would be the same size as 40 yoga mats. Imagine if our breaths were performed deeply, consciously and regularly throughout the day. Think how much more health, energy and vitality we could be creating within our bodies by practising simple breathing exercises. Think how much more clearly we'd think and how better we'd feel. These exercises allow the torso, ribs and throat to experience the full benefits of a breath and, as a result, our nervous system is balanced and so is our mind.

The practice of simply regulating our breath throughout the day creates changes that we almost can't comprehend. It opens up and releases any energetic blockages within our bodies so that any dormant energy within us is able to flow.

Breathing fully and rhythmically through the nose is important, because it sends air into the brain, the pituitary gland, the eyes and the palate of the mouth, which is directly linked to the nervous system. Simply focusing on breathing into our bellies and exhaling to the end of the breath has the potential to lift us out of depression, balance our hormones, regulate our periods, heal our digestion and elimination, bring us back to the present, and helps us to let go. All it requires is our effort and awareness because we've learned for many years how to *not* breathe. And the best part is, it's completely free.

***

The **PRACTICE**:

1. Inhale through your nose, feeling your diaphragm expand (down and outwards from the bottom of your ribs). Feel your belly fill with air.

2. Now on the exhale, see your belly contract, your diaphragm come to meet at the bottom of your ribs again whilst the air exhales through your nose.

3. Count to 6 on the inhale, and to 6 on the exhale. If you can't do 6 counts for now, just do what you can, focusing on your belly moving and the inhale and exhale being the same length.

4. If it helps, imagine you're letting go with each breathe. Feel any tension dissolve. It's all about releasing. Even if we're not exactly sure what we need to release. This is where we go past the mind, because the body intuitively knows what to do.

RECONNECT YOU, TO YOU

Through the regulation of our breath, we're able to calm ourselves down. In the peace zone, we're able to reconnect to our power because we're reconnecting to ourselves. It's our opportunity to go within and reconnect to the present moment. The amazing part is our mind naturally begins to take the hint and follows the steady rhythm and intention of our breath and our thoughts begin to calm down and become naturally more positive too. This is why it starts with the breath, not our minds.

BODY: SUMMARY

* The power of regulating our breath is underestimated. Firstly, we're brought back to the present moment and back within our bodies. This reconnects us to our power so that we're not just reacting to life. We begin to approach life from a calm, confident and centred perspective where we're aware of our strength and potential. This means what we think, feel, believe and perceive changes. And this completely changes our experience of life

* We know if we're stressed if we're breathing in a constricted way into our chests, or hardly breathing at all. We know if we're feeling more peaceful and connected if we're breathing into our bellies in a steady rhythm. Our breath is a key indicator as to what's going on within our mind. If we check in on how our breathing is at regular intervals throughout the day, we can create a new habit of optimal belly breathing and we have the opportunity to greatly improve our mental and physical health and rebalance our energy

* The tension in our body is created through chronic stress, which impacts our breathing and all the functions and processes of our body are affected to. Any nudges our body sends us are a gift, because

they're asking us to review how we're living. They're asking us to reconnect to ourselves so that we let go of pressure, urgency and not-enoughness and instead begin to appreciate our lives, so that we can see the beauty and grace all around us.

THE **BODY / MIND** LINK

Balance is a state of mind which manifests itself physically, so if we're mentally out of balance, we experience a reaction within our body. ASICS, the Japanese athletic company, has a fabulous acronym which explains the link between mind and body perfectly. The Latin phrase 'anima sana in corpore sano' translates as 'a sound mind in a sound body, or 'a healthy mind in a healthy body'. Our body suffers just enough so we don't realise the power of the mind. The body's suffering is a mask which hides the real source of our pain which exists within our mind. Our mental pain and despair is demonstrating our vulnerability and the aim of all of the chaos and drama we create - the playing it small, the lovelessness thinking and defences we build – is to hide the one thing from our awareness that we're longing to experience: the Truth about who we are and the absolute brilliance within us.

The act of regulating our breathing helps to bring the mind back under our control as opposed to allowing it to control us, which can cause havoc if left to its own devices. If we're living with an issue in the body, something that's out of balance, instead of asking for the body to be healed, we ask for the source of the problem to be healed. Which is something that's going on within our mind. The answer to our problem doesn't lie in an expensive remedy that we're promised will fix us, or in travelling the world to 'find and fix ourselves'. The answer to our problem lies in accessing what lies beneath our busy, frantic mind.

And now we've worked on breathing deeply and consciously first, we're able to get there faster making our mindset work even more profound.

So now we've done the breath work and brought ourselves down a little, let's go even further…

Are you ready to go deeper…?

THE NOT-SO MISSING PIECE
YOUR **MIND**
(BUT **DEEPER**)

***

When you close your eyes and become aware of what's happening within your mind, what do you notice? Try it now. Close your eyes and tune in to what's going on. Normally we begin to notice an incessant buzzing noise like a computer firing up and the busyness of thoughts constantly whirling around our heads. It's enough to make us want to open our eyes! It's no wonder we avoid meditating at times. Trying to get past all of this noise and change our thoughts can seem like the hardest thing in the world to do, but this isn't the part of the mind we're interested in working on.

At the very centre of our minds, below all of the relentless activity, is where our actual mind is located. What we think of as our mind, is just noise. It's our conscious mind, the part where we're always trying to work out what's going on and it's where we react to life. But deep deep *deep* down below all of this noise and confusion is where our actual mind is. And it's this part we'll access in this chapter. This is the part of our mind where all of our power is and it's the foundation from which we are able to build our house upon a rock. It's where our affirmations become facts because they take root, and it's where our mindset work makes a profound difference because we're accessing a different part of our mind than we normally reach.

So how do we get there?

Surrounding our mind and clouding our vision is a whirlwind of thoughts and activity which does everything it can to stop us from ever getting there. But beyond this cloudiness, is our light. Which if you're anything like me, the word 'light' used to turn me off. I'd think: "Here's another crazy person talking about light!" Our light isn't anything woo woo. Our light is simply the Truth about us; the person we're capable of being, the best side we've got. It's the opposite of the darkness within us, where we can be crabby, depressed and anxious. What meditation helps us work through is our resistance to showing up with all we've got - if we do it right.

If you were to take an honest and thorough look inside of your mind at the thoughts which seem to occupy your thinking, it's highly likely the majority of these thoughts are related to what's happened (or not) in the past, to anxieties in the present or to fears about the future. At times, our thoughts aren't even our own. Thoughts of anger, hurt and resentment from the past, or thoughts of uncertainty, fear, potential illness, loss, limitation and death in the future seem to occupy our minds more frequently than thoughts of perfect security and complete fulfilment. Which sounds amazing doesn't it?! Imagine spending more of your waking hours feeling secure, loving and fulfilled.

THE SOLUTION

The problem is fear and getting past it seems to be a never ending task. *A Course in Miracles* teaches us that the only way we can overcome our fears is through the mastery of love. *Love? Really?* It sounds so alien when we've been dwelling in a constant fight or flight mindset. What it's teaching us is that when we turn on a light within us, the darkness disappears. Yet the problem with most mindset work is that it doesn't go deep enough because it's only working at a superficial level.

Most mindset work is aimed at always changing the effects, if we're lucky it asks us to go a little deeper, whereas the Course asks us to go straight to the root cause. The cause is always inside of us and when we approach mindset work with a different intention, the results dramatically change. It's harder to try and change the effects without changing the cause first, and that's why we can try so hard for so long and feel like we're taking one step forward and two back.

If we spend our energy trying to master eliminating fear, then all we're doing is asserting its power over us. We know what we focus on expands, so focusing on what we fear, how the fear came about, and how we can go about eliminating it, means our experience in life is always the same. If we're always trying to erase our fears then we'll always have fears to erase. If we're always trying to work out how we got our fears and who we can blame for them, then we'll always remain stuck. This is a very stressful place to live, especially when Buddha tells us our life is all about our thoughts, which stresses us out even further because we just can't seem to break the cycle.

On an intellectual level we can understand why we're scared of success, because we've been taught to not be too big for our boots. We can understand why we're scared of totally loving someone if we've been hurt in the past. We can understand why we're scared of death, because of the pain we've experienced in the past through loss. And we can appreciate why we're scared of failing, being rejected or laughed at, but it's not helping us overcome it all.

MIND: EXERCISE

In Lesson 26 of *A Course in Miracles* (W-p1.26), we're asked to monitor what we're thinking about for a whole day, which reveals a lot about our current mindset. On some level we know our mind leans towards negativity and fear, but in regularly acknowledging our thoughts we see just how much effort we waste on wrong thinking.

Let's work through it together. Close your eyes and spend a minute or so searching your mind and consider what's occupying your thoughts.

I am concerned about…

For example, you may be thinking about a worry, a problem, a fear, a threat, your health, or money. Maybe you're thinking about someone who pissed you off yesterday, last year, or ten years ago. Maybe you're feeling anxious or inadequate. Maybe you're worrying about something that's happened, something that might happen or something that isn't happening and should be. You might be overly-concerned about your body or your future. If you're harbouring some sort of resentment against someone, you might say:

"I'm concerned about an argument I had with my neighbour yesterday, who was really bitchy with me."

Now spend a minute or so thinking about what happened.

What are you afraid of?

How do you feel?

For example: *"I'm afraid she might do it again. I'm afraid I didn't speak up for myself enough. I'm afraid I look weak. I'm afraid she thinks she's better than me. I'm afraid to meet her again. I'm afraid she'll blow up again. I'm angry at her. I'm pissed off with her. How dare she speak to me like that! How dare she tell me what to do! I'm angry at myself for being nervous. I'm angry at myself for not getting all of my points across. I'm angry, full stop."*

Can you see where our thinking can go, lost in the hurt? These thoughts are not helping us process what happened and they're not helping us to get it off our chests. Nor are they successfully passing the blame onto the other person. These thoughts are actually attacking *us*, because they're attacking *our* peace of mind. And these thoughts can go on for hours, days, and even years and all they do is drain our energy and lower our vibe.

OUR CRAZY THINKING

This low-level thinking occupies so much airtime throughout the day and if we come back to this exercise regularly it's staggering to realise how much mental energy we waste on negative thinking by dwelling in the past or worrying about the future. The thoughts which attack us are fearful and chaotic and they affect our peace of mind because they knock us out of our centre and take us out of the present, which is where our power is. They take us from our natural core position of peace right into the depths of our loveless thinking. All of the goodness and love from the entire Universe is available to us every day, but we block it out by holding onto hurt or resentment. And then we wonder why our life isn't working.

We're taught in A Course in Miracles that: *"There are no idle thoughts. All thought creates form on some level".* (T-2.VI. 9:13) That's great when we're thinking with love, but not so great when we're not. If we're not proactively filling our minds with light, the darkness sets in. Thoughts loop around our brains continuously and if we're not feeding our mind with positivity and potential then we'll be feeding it with negative and limited thoughts, and those two mindsets create completely opposing results. So how do we change all of this? Because if you're anything like me, you've tried to change your thoughts with little success.

And here's the key:

WHAT OUR LOVELESS-NESS IS ACTUALLY HIDING

Although we don't like feeling fear, being overwhelmed with feelings of inadequacy, or getting lost in our crazy, loveless thinking, we're not totally comfortable completely removing those thoughts and feelings either, because underneath all the hurt and despair we might find something we fear even more - **the person we are capable of being.**

Yep, it's under there. Under all of the noise and distractions.

And that's what we're going to reach.

We've become comfy dwelling in the crucification, the pain and suffering, more than in the resurrection - the light and Truth. We're more comfy dwelling in our weaknesses than contemplating the magnitude of love and strength hidden beneath them. We're not terrified of failing, we're actually really terrified of how great we could be, because the Truth asks us to step up and we're not sure we're good enough, worthy enough, or ready for that.

So whilst affirmations and mindset work does change us, if we're not getting to the root of the problem and dealing with our sense of inadequacy and vulnerability first - then we're only scratching the surface.

SO WHAT DO WE DO?
THE PERMANENT FIX

We may have been paralysed by our weaknesses in the past, but now we can use this to our advantage, because the opposite to our fear and doubt is where all our power lies. So we can take comfort in that, because if our fear has been so debilitating and life sucking, stopping us from pursuing our dreams and being the person we're capable of being, then the opposite to that must be our greatness, our power, everything we desire, plus the ability to achieve it. It's like a pendulum. If we've been low then there's more to come, because there's a high waiting for us around the corner. If there was no fear, we would remember how freakin' amazing we are - all of the time, but we're afraid of love, because we're really afraid of living life. If we're looking for a permanent fix then we've found it. This is where all of mindset work suddenly falls into place and becomes a heck of a lot easier.

THE ANSWER

It's possible to reach a state where we're brave enough and bold enough to finally conquer our fears, because we've reached a point where we're so unhappy not expressing our potential, we end up with no other option. We do this not through our physical effort, because we access our power in direct proportion to our willingness to surrender. This means surrendering to the notion of there being a power greater than ourselves, an invisible intelligence which has the power to self-correct when it seems like the forces of darkness have beaten us down.

And we can relate to this power however we feel comfortable using whatever words resonate with us. Some people call it the Universe, source, God, creator, light, a power, Mary, Buddha, Allah and many other names. But ultimately they all mean the same thing. And to me they all mean love because if we break it down to the basics: "God is love." It's not a man sat in a chair high above us who answers our requests or not, depending upon how well behaved we've been, or not! God is love. A feeling we can choose to experience inside ourselves, or not, because we can also choose to block it instead.

Something keeps calling us to remember the love and brilliance within us and our potential which is lying dormant. This 'something' won't go away and we should be grateful for that. Eventually we'll listen and eventually we'll take notice, but it's entirely up to us how long it takes for us to acknowledge it. Sometimes we let it take three months, three years, three decades, or sometimes an entire lifetime.

***

LET'S ACCESS WHAT LIES BENEATH

It's taken me years to understand that everything we're looking for is already within us. It would really annoy me when I first heard teachers say this, because I didn't understand what that meant. I'd be like: "I know I often feel inadequate, low and anxious. I know I'm not in a job I love, that I really should have more savings and my health could be better. I rarely feel much love and gratitude and I know I'm holding back in life but I don't know what to do about it." I knew all of this was inside of me but I was unaware what else was there. So if we look beyond all of this suffering we can find that person we're capable of being. The secure, happy, loving and loveable version. The version that's good enough. The perfect, complete, strong, powerful and unlimited version. And there's a way of accessing this every day.

MEDITATION...
BUT NOT AS WE KNOW IT

There are so many books on meditation and it seems so intimidating to learn, but I found that they don't actually teach us *how* to meditate. It's not complicated, it's not religious and it doesn't have to be spiritual. What's blocking us experiencing and knowing our brilliance is something meditation can move through. We won't experience it through our own effort, we'll experience it through a spiritual awakening. And while that sounds super impressive, it's actually an everyday occurrence. What it means in its most basic form is that we're awakening to the fact that we're more than we ever thought we could be and we're becoming motivated to experience it more often than not.

ALTERING OUR CONSCIOUSNESS

When we deliberately alter our consciousness in any way, we're trying to find ourselves and experience bliss. We're seeking our highest Self - the part of us who knows who it is and why it's here. We achieve a similar feeling through the high of a party drug, where we feel love for everyone and everything and we believe we can be more, feel more and love more. We feel amazing, unlimited, and indestructible, but if we're achieving this through artificial means, we then have to be prepared for the come down on the other side. Mediation on the other hand, seems like much more effort, and at the outset it may potentially seem more boring, but what meditation doesn't have is the crash the next day.

Western philosophers used their intellect whereas ancient sages used personal experience to reach beyond normal levels of consciousness. By moving our attention away from the body and the conscious mind, we access a deeper level of our consciousness than we usually do and experience love as being within us rather than outside of us. When we escape the limits of the body and the mind through letting go, we move into another realm, a realm where nothing is impossible. Another term for this is Heaven, which is a state of infinite possibility.

THE INCREDIBLE POWER OF OUR MIND

Meditation shrinks the part of our brain that's linked to fear, anxiety and depression. Yet it's often dismissed, because its power isn't felt until it's practised on a regular basis. What we're aiming to do is to train our minds to reach this deeper aspect of ourselves every day. The untrained mind comes in and out of meditation, while the trained mind moves beyond the distractions because it's experienced lovelessness for too long and desperately wants to feel the opposite.

THE SECRETS TO MEDITATION...

WHAT I WISHED SOMEONE HAD TAUGHT ME YEARS AGO

1. When we initially sit down to try and meditate we can become overwhelmed with the noise and disturbance which is constantly whirling around inside of our heads, which only appears to get louder the harder we try to clear our minds. The aim isn't to clear our mind. The aim is to simply go within, which takes the pressure off us straight away.

2. What we focus on whilst we're meditating matters. Instead of focusing on clearing the mind or 'finding' peace, focus instead on your heart and feeling it grow. Feel your heart triple in size. This keeps your attention within you and away from unnecessary distractions.

3. Before we sit down to meditate, we should be aware of our state. Are we anxious, stressed or angry? The mood we're in when we enter meditation has a huge impact on what happens during it. If we go in feeling angry, we'll create more of the same throughout the session. Too often we sit down to meditate with the weight of the world on our shoulders. The aim obviously isn't to enter meditation like a zen monk, but rather to let go of how we're feeling so we're open to receive a new kind of energy that'll uplift and transform us.

4. We think the power to help us comes from outside of us, when it's all within us. So we can keep the attention within us by keeping our chin tilted downwards slightly towards our heart, keeping our eyes closed so we go within and focus on being with ourselves in the moment.

5. If you hear noises or sounds around you, that's ok. I used to want the perfect place to meditate but anywhere will do. As long as we're focused on going within, eventually the outside noises won't be a problem. It can help to focus the eyes on the space between the eyebrows. It's amazing how much activity goes on with our eyes, even when our eyes are closed. Keeping them focused helps the mind to focus.

6. It's helpful to start by seeing a small golden ball of light within the very centre of your mind. Think of this ball of light as your actual mind, your real mind beyond the fear, to strengthen the connection to our hearts, the strength and power within us. It also helps to see a small ball of golden light within your heart. This focus helps when we become distracted to bring us back to the present moment. Some

people like to use mantras and find those helpful like repeating the words "let go" or "release". Some people prefer to visualise any thoughts which come up to just float by. Use whatever works for you to stay connected within yourself.

Then enjoy, and watch the magic happen.

MIND: SUMMARY

*   Our ego would love us to live in fear and never reach our potential but our smaller self is breaking free from these chains because we're starting to remember what we're capable of. Underneath the busyness and fears which consume our thoughts is the person we know we can be

*   Meditation moves us beyond the craziness to the love and potential that lies beyond. Instead of reaching for the coffee, cake or wine, close your eyes and go within. When you do this consistently it becomes an incredibly powerful, refreshing and energising tool.

*   Whenever we're depressed, anxious or feeling inadequate, it's because we've chosen to dwell in the wrong mindset, but it's not as easy as saying 'snap out of it'. It's not as easy as saying we need to choose a different mindset or pick new thoughts. We need the tools to help us do that and in the next chapter, we'll look at what is directly impacting our mindset in any given moment.

They say it all starts with the mind, but personally, I've found it starts with what's going on (or not) at a deeper level within our hearts which directly impacts what's going on within our mind.

So any idea where we're going to next…?!

MISSING PIECE NO 2
YOUR **HEART**

***

I struggled to write the opening to this chapter, it felt too emotional and too raw because the impact of having a closed heart affects us to a degree we almost can't comprehend. The impact it has on every area of our lives is significant - it holds us back, keeps us down and restricts our life on every level. It causes chaos and craziness in our home and work life, it affects our health, our wealth and our happiness and it affects how well we express ourselves, or not.

By the end of this chapter, if you do the exercises, then any mindset work you do afterwards becomes *profound*. If you've tried tapping whilst looking in the mirror saying: "I love myself" 100 times a day and it's not worked as well as it should. If you've ever wondered why you don't feel as loving as you sense you could, then this chapter will clear out everything from the past to allow you to move forward.

We didn't wake up one morning and intend to reject ourselves or other people. It's not a rational thought, it's a subconscious, automatic response to life. Someone once hurt us and we do everything we can to protect ourselves from it ever happening again. And what we really want is to fall in love with ourselves and other people, all over again. Somehow life teaches us to hold love back because there's not enough to go around, so we hold onto every scrap of it that we can. And the biggest belief of all, is that we might not be good enough or deserving enough to experience total unconditional love for ourselves or towards others.

The world teaches us to go out there and 'get' more love which is always focused on us getting love from someone or something outside of us. Or we're bombarded with memes telling us that we need to love ourselves first. And whilst it's not necessarily completely incorrect advice, it's approaching the situation from an onerous angle. It's causing us to overlook a fundamental key to truly unlocking the love that's already within us. Sometimes it means we miss the experience all together. And there's an easier way to experience it all.

A more enlightened perspective is to know *how* we experience love. The problem isn't that love doesn't exist - the problem lies in how often *we* connect to this love within us, how often *we* bring this love to others, and whether we're willing to remove the blocks which prevents us from doing this. We have the power to create an unlimited amount of love but we hold back, waiting for other people to make us happy, or deciding if they deserve our love or not. Our hearts yearn to give love to others so we can actually experience it, even though we resist doing this on so many levels.

It makes me laugh to think how spiritual I thought I was becoming by praying, meditating, practising yoga and drinking organic green juice, but then I would spend most of my waking hours harbouring resentments, subtly judging people, having unloving thoughts and feelings towards people, hoping they would change and stop behaving the way they do so I could be happy. It turns out, after many years of research, that it's a pretty ineffective approach!

THE 'NOT SO SEXY' ANSWER
TO OUR LOVELESSNESS

I started to learn of a way to clear out all of the baggage from the past which promised to be the key. The only problem was, I'd heard this kind of promise before and it hadn't worked and the approach I was learning didn't sound very exciting. If anything, it sounded too simple. Surely I needed to go off, spend thousands again seeking the best gurus, travelling the world to find the best healer? This way was telling me I could do it in my own front room. And here's the message:

The love within us is experienced in direct proportion to our willingness to *forgive*.

There it is. The answer. I told you it wasn't so sexy!

Tell me I'm not the only one whose first thought was: "It can't be that simple!" and "I don't have anyone or anything to forgive." It's only when I started to do the work that I realised I did.

The trouble is, forgiveness doesn't sound like it will have that much impact. *A Course in Miracles* explains that forgiveness is the fundamental key to us achieving the inner peace we're dreaming of. If there's a disturbance in our hearts, or a place where we're not totally at peace, then it's the Universe's way of speaking to us and guiding us back to the love within ourselves. The place we resist so much.

Forgiveness offers us everything we want: happiness, a sense of purpose, peace of mind, and awareness of our potential.

Forgiveness offers quietness, gentleness, comfort and rest. It is the end of suffering and the answer to our pain.

Forgiveness brings us the money and success we desire and removes the blocks to allow our life to finally take off.

When we let other people off the hook and stop focusing on their perceived flaws, we open up the way to just love them instead. When we forgive people, we change on a level we can't comprehend. We believe that if we give love to others, we'll have less for ourselves but the love we give to others isn't lost, and it doesn't mean our store of love has been depleted; the law of forgiveness means that we receive back exactly what we've given, and more. Which can be a blessing and a curse depending upon what we've put out there. A wise lady once said to me: "If you'd just start giving more love, you'd receive a tonne of love back". And it worked. Once I'd gotten over my walls of resistance.

A Course in Miracles isn't the only spiritual text which deals with forgiveness, or lack of. We've been taught about its power since Biblical times. The Lord's Prayer contains two affirmations which we repeat without really considering what they mean or the power they contain:

1. Forgive us our debtors = *means* = Forgive me for where I have got it wrong and made a mistake. (And who hasn't?!)

2. As we forgive those who have debts against us = *means* = help me forgive others where they've made a mistake.

That's it.

It's nothing elaborate or overly religious, and it's nothing stuffy or out of our control. It's actually a very simple concept. So if it's so powerful and accessible, why don't we practise it? Because we know if we did, we'd receive everything we're searching for and the pain of the search seems more comfortable and familiar to us than accepting the peace of mind we could have instead.

Forgiveness means we'd naturally be stepping into our greatness and into the person we're capable of being and that freaks us out even more than staying as we are. If we don't practise forgiveness, then we don't receive the miracles that are offered to us on a daily basis. If we're not getting answers and life isn't working for us like we want it to, then we're asked to thoroughly check ourselves, with complete honesty, for the places within ourselves where we're holding on to a grievance and thinking without love.

"And whenever you stand praying, if you have anything against anyone, forgive him."
Mark 11:25

Spiritual power struggles to pass through a mind which is holding on to resentment or grievances. Hate - however subtly felt and even disguised as being a 'fair evaluation' of someone - prevents the flow of spiritual power. When we've experienced a sense of fear, foreboding, anxiety, depression or any negative state of mind and we've taken an honest look inside our hearts at the resentments, hate or anger we're holding onto, forgiveness is the key to us experiencing the complete opposite. It's an open door to our wholeness, where Heaven is awaiting us and where our Higher Self resides.

HOW TO PRACTISE FORGIVENESS
(When we think we don't need to, or we don't really want to)

Lesson 78 in *A Course in Miracles* (W-p1.78) focuses specifically on how we can replace the grievances we're holding onto with a miracle instead. A miracle isn't always as obvious as winning the lottery - it can be a small shift in our perception, the tiniest upliftment in our thinking which, if we've been low, we welcome with open arms.

This lesson we'll work through encourages us to look deeply into our hearts and minds to see what kind of grievances we're holding onto. It's easy to think we don't hold any grievances and we don't have anyone or anything to forgive. It's only when we work through the lesson that it reveals how many grievances we do actually hold towards nearly everyone we know, and even the tiniest of those grievances is blocking a miracle. These grievances might be feelings of resentment, hate or anger, a small annoyance, a minor frustration, or complete betrayal and injustice.

HEART: EXERCISE
NO. 1:

1. Think about people who you hold what seems to be a
    major grievance against.

Perhaps someone has let you down, said something you
don't agree with, or behaved in a way you didn't like.
Perhaps someone has angered, frustrated, hurt or annoyed
you. Perhaps someone cheated on you, left you, or abused
you. Perhaps someone bullied you, behaved unfairly at
work, stole from you, or deceived you. It could be a family
member, an ex, your neighbour, a colleague, a business
partner, a client, a tenant, a tradesman or a hairdresser. It
could be the person who took your parking space this
morning or cut you up in traffic, or the person who got in
your way or spoke to you abruptly. Maybe it's that guy in
your office who annoys you, or the woman who never
completes her work to the standard you require. Maybe you
feel judged by someone for how you're living your life. This
could have been yesterday, last month or 20 years ago.

Whoever has come to mind, is the one. If there's more than
one person, that's absolutely fine (and completely normal.)

2. Now think about a situation or event that you hold a
grievance against.

Maybe it's a grievance about the economy, taxes, the
government, institutions, religion, laws, rules, the media, the
world, God, social media, parents, partners, friends,
siblings, your hometown, your education, roadworks, traffic,
or the expectations you feel are placed on you.

3. Now run through an image in your mind of everyone you
know standing on a catwalk. Scan the line of everyone on
the stage. Notice what grievances, what annoyances and

what resentments you hold, however small, about everyone on there.

***

THE RESULT

If you're anything like me, the first time you run through this exercise you'll see it's a real eye-opener. I was shocked to discover that I had some form of grievance with nearly everyone and everything I could think of – my neighbours, my pets, my husband (many times!), my family, friends, companies, regulations, society, the way God had been explained to me, Facebook, Instagram, money, ex-boyfriends, ex-bosses, colleagues, school, my hometown, the guy walking too slowly in front of me, the neighbour who leaves her things lying around - the list goes on.

It's mind-blowing when we realise the sheer number of grievances, minor irritations and annoyances we're unknowingly holding on to. If you're now panicking that you've blocked numerous blessings don't worry, because the miracles we've blocked aren't lost. They're stored for us until the day we're ready to receive them and we can to do that right away through forgiveness.

WHERE THE F*** DO I START...?

With so much to forgive and let go of, it seems like we'd need to constantly monitor our thoughts, which would completely sap all of our energy and would become a full-time job. A daily practice keeps us aware of any grievances and allows us to release them quickly, without letting them build up. We don't have to forgive everyone or everything when we start forgiveness, we're just asked to make a sincere start. A daily reflection on how we've shown up, reacted and behaved isn't boring, it's necessary to secure an emotional foundation of inner peace. We're setting up each day for success, starting within us, which is the most powerful place we can be when we're practising forgiveness (or the most distressing place to be when we're not). By doing this deep inner clearing out work within our hearts, our mental state is naturally uplifted. Can you see why saying an affirmation doesn't have the same impact if we're still carrying hurts, pain and resentments in our hearts? It's like an internal battle, a daily tug of war. And we lose each time if we don't do the forgiveness work first.

THE PERSON WE FORGET TO FORGIVE

I was speaking to a client one day who was going through some 'stuff'. Jenny was 35, single and while she'd had many boyfriends and casual flings, she'd still not met 'the one'. Her friends were all getting married, so the pressure to meet Mr Right was growing. She'd been in enough therapists' chairs to know that she'd spent years trying to manufacture more love in her life. She'd desperately been searching for someone and she was feeling increasingly empty when a man left or didn't call back.

As we talked about the principles in this book, she recognised that love couldn't have abandoned her, because that wasn't possible. It was just temporarily covered by the hurt, the disappointment, the betrayal and the sense of inadequacy she'd bought into. She wasn't aware of exactly when her issues had started, but as a child she didn't feel good enough, as a young adult she'd been humiliated by an ex-boyfriend, and she knew she'd made some mistakes along the way. These experiences had turned into her personality characteristics and behaviour. It took her years to understand what was going on.

She'd spent years working on her mindset. She's said every affirmation ever created. And the answer finally came through forgiveness which isn't an intellectual process, it's a process which occurs inside our hearts. It's easier to blame other people for what's happened to us and blame them for why we behave the way we do. Yet when we're thinking of who or what to forgive, we often overlook the one person we have to forgive who would bring us immediate release, and that one person is: **ourselves.**

By forgiving the people she felt had hurt her, the situations she'd experienced, and forgiving herself for her part in the drama, Jenny's life was transformed. We often think our part in a situation is small and place more emphasis on the person who has hurt us. Even if our part is small, we're encouraged to go within us to understand our behaviour. In Jenny's case, why did she keep giving her number out to men she knew would mistreat her or never call back? Why was she constantly looking for a man who she knew would reject her, leave her, or cheat on her? Why was she putting herself in this position time and time again?

The reason comes down to the lack of belief Jenny had in herself. We assume we'll naturally 'get over' our sense of inadequacy by a certain age, only to still have those feelings into our 30s, 40s and beyond. Jenny's sense of inadequacy was an aspect of her personality she could overcome through forgiveness, because she'd let go of the hurt which would mean she could experience the love within her instead. So she didn't need to generate more belief in herself, which, if you've ever tried, you'll know is a painstaking process. She just needed to let go of the baggage she'd accumulated over the years so she could finally be the person she knew she could be.

FORGIVING OTHERS

Another client overheard a conversation where her boyfriend's friend asked him: "Do you think she's good enough for you?" Gemma's heart sank. Every time she met this friend, her sense of inadequacy quickly returned and affected how she interacted with him. She also found herself not feeling good enough when he was around. She felt small and anxious, would blush if he asked her a question, and she felt he never seemed to listen to her and cut her off mid-sentence. This situation happened 10 years ago and she was still holding on to those emotions today.

If someone holds a space for us to be brilliant and to shine, we subconsciously feel their blessing and - more often than not - we do shine. When someone is watching and waiting for us to make a mistake because they don't think we're good enough, we feel this vibe and it knocks us out of our power. So what's the answer? Blame the other person and hold on to the hurt for another 10 years? Blame herself for her feelings of inadequacy? Try and overcome it by repeating affirmation telling her she's good enough? She'd tried that and it hadn't worked.

As simple as it sounds, Gemma knew she needed to forgive the friend, although it felt much more satisfying to hate him. As a spiritual seeker, we're asked to stand in the middle of the darkness and be the light. We're not being sanctimonious or pretending the hurt didn't happen. We're choosing to transcend the upset because we want more than anything to be happy and at peace and we know we have the power to transform any relationship when we transform ourselves first, through our practice of forgiveness.

Even though every voice in her head screamed at her that he should be the one apologising, Gemma forgave the friend. After all, her hurt wasn't affecting him, it was just bringing her down. If we were to look deeply into the psyche of the friend, we'd uncover his own feelings of inadequacy, which is why he recognised them in Gemma in the first place. As we've learnt, what we perceive in someone else is just an unhealed aspect of our own personality. If we focused only on seeing the good in someone, then that's what we'd see, but we're in the habit of seeing someone as limited and not good enough. We don't recognise the unlimited potential within them, because we're not recognising it in ourselves first.

WHAT WE'RE ACTUALLY REJECTING

When we fall in love with someone, we're literally in Heaven on Earth, because we choose to see only the good in them. The other person is free to be who they are - there is no control, judgement, neediness or blame. This isn't an illusion. This is the Truth, the possibility. Over time we've been trained to focus on what we perceive to be people's mistakes and flaws. We notice behaviours, actions and words that we don't agree with. We blame people, we judge them, we hold things against them for something they may have said or done years ago. We get frustrated with them. We subtly control them, put them down and we wonder if they're good enough. Rejecting our partner though, or any relationship, is really a way of rejecting God, because it's a way of rejecting all of the love that's available to us, however subconscious our behaviour appears to be.

We have to ask ourselves: why are we pushing love away? Is it too good? Does it feel uncomfortable? Do we know how to maintain the love we're feeling? Do we feel we deserve it, or not? We're asked to only see the good in others - to see the light or the love in them and to see the good in them. We're asked to see beyond the illusion of our opinion of them and only see the good and of course, to forgive, forgive, forgive. By doing that we open ourselves up to start living in a different world.

If we can't see the good in everyone then we're not seeing the good within ourselves and we feel disconnected and disempowered. Proactively looking for the good in others by speaking kind words about them and understanding how we're all connected is where our happiness lies. And sometimes we're not sure we're ready for that.

In any interaction, it helps if we ask ourselves:

What am I giving?

and

What am I _not_ giving?

If we ask within, we'll be shown why we're withholding love.

What am I giving? Is it judgement, blame, annoyance or greed? These thoughts and feelings are within us, not the other person. They only impact us. Every thought we send out is logged by the Universe and appears as the result of our lives. So if something isn't working as we want it to, we now know where to look. This is placing ourselves firmly as the 'cause' - which can take years for us to accept.

What am I _not_ giving? Is it patience, love, gentleness, or compassion?

We spend so much time focusing on what someone doesn't do, as opposed to all the things they actually do. Many people end relationships to find someone else who can provide that missing 20% they feel their partner lacks without even realising they're leaving behind 80% of greatness.

THE REAL PROBLEM IN RELATIONSHIPS

When we have an issue with someone, we think the problem is what they're doing to us. They may be obnoxious, condescending or judgemental, but the problem isn't that someone is judging us, the problem is that we then judge them back. If I say: "I'm hurt by their condescending or judgemental behaviour," what's really happened is they've closed their hearts to us and we quickly and unconsciously close our hearts to them. It's so immediate and instinctive we don't even realise what we're doing, but we know something is wrong because we don't feel good and the relationship feels strained. Even if they hurt us, or they 'started' it, it doesn't matter. Our personality might be bruised and we might feel offended or hurt, but from an enlightened perspective, we know that if someone isn't showing us love it's just because they're crying out for it themselves.

Maybe there's something about us that triggers them. Maybe they're intimidated by our age, looks, credentials or possibility, and they just can't deal with it. The way they act usually stems from something that happened to them in their childhood and we trigger them, even without us knowing it. And we might never know why. We're all just acting and reacting to the experiences we've been through and the scars we've picked up along the way, but we don't need to engage with this low-level drama. Our life will change as soon as we decide to change.

IT'S ALL ABOUT US

The responsibility is always on us, even though our ego tries to make us blame someone else. If only they behaved in a different way, we'd be happy. If only they were happier, less judgmental, less condescending, or less obnoxious, then we'd be happy.

We're always delaying our happiness and placing it in the future. We say we'll be happy when someone else changes, but this just prevents us from healing. It's a trap. The ego is alive and kicking. It's surviving because we're placing the blame outside ourselves, so we're not healing on the level of cause. If we actually dwelled in the relationship in a place of complete acceptance and love for the other person, we would experience true Heaven on Earth, our ego would disappear, and all would be love.

People will always judge us. Some people will like us and others won't. People won't always behave in the way we want them to. We can't control that; we can only control ourselves. It saves us days, weeks - maybe even years of torment obsessing about other people's behaviours. We're asked to rise above it. To fly above it. Don't spend valuable energy dwelling there. We're being encouraged to raise our thoughts and feelings upwards and to rise above the suffering and chaos.

WHAT OUR GRIEVANCES ARE REALLY HIDING

We can obsess about other people's shortcomings, but a grievance is just a mask to hide the pain we feel within ourselves. If we're focusing on what we think someone should do differently or how they're not good enough, it's a way for our ego to divert the attention away from us. If our attention is focused on how someone doesn't meet our expectations then we can't heal, so we stay in tune with our ego (our lovelessness) and nothing changes.

When we let go of the perceived shortcomings of others we can see the love inside them instead, which means we remember the love within ourselves. Except we're not sure we're ready to remember to do that. The ego is afraid of love and does everything it can to 'protect' us from feeling it, because it knows if we really knew joy, the ego would become irrelevant. In other words, if we really knew love, we would know our greatness and then we'd be happy.

THE **HEART** / **SPIRIT** LINK

*   We searched the world for the love we thought we were lacking but it's been right inside of us all along and forgiveness of ourselves and others is the way to unlock this love, so it can become our experience.

68

* There are no limits to the love we could feel inside of us, but we have to practise forgiveness in order to remove the blocks we hold around our hearts

* Forgiveness offers us everything we want. Holding a grievance of any size blocks our good and forgiveness allows miracles to be released to us instead

* In any encounter we should always ask ourselves what we're giving, or not giving. The onus is always on ourselves, even though our ego tempts us to blame everyone else. We have the power to transform our relationships and our lives so that we can make a significant contribution in the world. We have the tool which enables us to overcome our lovelessness and release our potential instead.

***

If forgiveness can bring us everything we've ever wanted: the health, the wealth and the happiness, suddenly it becomes a lot more appealing. Now we've cleared up what we've been holding onto, we've opened ourselves up for everything good to come to us and we're ready to start allowing it in.

I'm sure you've read about manifesting your dreams. All you need to do is ask for what you want and it'll appear. It sounds super easy and magical but what if it doesn't work like we're told it will? What if you have no idea what to ask for? What if you have no idea who to ask?

After stumbling around for years trying to work it all out, I had to go deeper with it all. And as you know me by now, it was an inside-out job. This is the place where everything changes.

It was time for an attitude adjustment…

MISSING PIECE NO 3
YOUR **SPIRIT**

***

There's a daily practice we can do that has the power to change everything. And once we know the secret to using it, it can seriously create magic. However, in order to tap into it, we must completely let go of what this particular word means to us and be open to relearning the subject again. I even thought about changing the word, but on reflection there's nothing actually wrong with the word itself. The practice is prayer and I know, it all sounds a bit boring but stick with me! The problem with prayer is with our association with it and what we think it requires us to do. This resistance has come from our early religious exposure, the time when we were taught the secrets to life but often in an upside down way. The practice itself doesn't have to be associated with religion. It's time to reinvent it and reclaim it for ourselves, so that we can start to benefit from everything it can offer us. If you've tried to manifest what you want, then here's the answer.

***

I'd heard about the power of prayer numerous times, but I'd never really embraced it. It always felt slightly alien to me. It felt too esoteric and I struggled to connect with it. I didn't know who or what I was talking to and I didn't know what to say or how to say it. I'd kind of mumble a few requests and hope they'd be instantly answered and was disappointed when they weren't. I wasn't sure it worked, and I wasn't convinced I was the right type of person to be praying. The majority of the time I became distracted and my mind would start racing through all sorts of thoughts, largely about things I didn't want to have happen. Most of the time I was asking for something outside of me to make me happier, and that's if I knew what to pray for at all.

WHAT IS PRAYER?

If you think about what a prayer is, it's positive thinking, visualisation, gratitude and affirmations, all in one go. It's like a one-stop spiritual practice shop. The power behind all of these combined practices is so immense it becomes a spiritual force. Prayer creates profound changes on the level of cause, which is the deepest level we can work on and it changes everything, because it works from the inside-out. It transforms us first and then it transforms our world. We're held back daily by our thinking, but the ultimate purpose of prayer is to change our thoughts, which as a result, changes our experiences.

Prayer can uplift us, change us and renew us like nothing else. Whatever we want, wants us, and prayer removes any blocks that are in the way. Prayer works on a higher realm than we normally have control over, because we tap into the supreme mind way down beyond all of the fear and it releases an invisible force that shatters limitations, it allows miracles to occur, and makes the impossible become totally possible.

It's a fascinating and powerful practice that doesn't get enough credit because its benefits can be hard to understand and accept. There's nothing complicated about it, but the main block we have is in our own conception of what it is and who we're praying to. If we can let go of our resistance then we'd access the power, peace and potential it contains. There's nothing dull about it either; it contains dynamic power that can make us irresistible to what we want.

When we pray we're connecting to an invisible, intelligent force that's always at work for our highest good and prayer allows us to plug right into that force. Through the act of praying our consciousness is expanded, so what we're able to receive expands too. Prayer releases the highest vibration of energy in and around us, working on our behalf to produce the right attitudes within us and therefore the right results. The more we turn to prayer the more it works, and we come to realise we have an almighty power within us wherever we go.

THE BIGGEST OBSTACLE TO OUR SUCCESS

What creates confusion is that we think we're praying to something outside of us in the distance, somewhere out in space. We think there's someone up there, deciding whether or not to answer our prayers based on how we've behaved.

With all this disconnection and judgement, it's no wonder we're not praying. If we were to get metaphysical about this and think about what we've learnt so far, we know that there's nothing outside of us. When we realise that what we're trying to reach is actually within us, we can direct our prayers straight there. This automatically makes our prayers more meaningful and powerful. Instead of just stumbling over a few words in an unmoving way, we switch on our feelings and emotions and start to pray with our entire body, heart and mind, which is a powerful combination. In this state, we have the power to move mountains.

The issue isn't that our prayers haven't been answered, the issue lies in how we're praying. We're normally asking for something to make us happier on the outside, but if we're honest we don't know what that something is. Asking from this mindset comes from a belief that we're lacking and this diminishes the power of prayer.

We've all chased things and felt deeply unhappy when we've received them. We've all asked for more without appreciating what we already have, but this intelligence within us does know what will make us happy and it knows the fastest way to get there. It's sat patiently waiting for us to stop controlling everything ourselves and let it get on with its work without us getting in the way. If we abandoned our own perception of what we think we want, and how and when it should appear, we'd open up the way for all the good to be released to us instead.

The problem is, praying doesn't seem that sexy or appealing. If we've only experienced it through a traditional church service where we've mumbled our way through a few prayers with little emotion, then we've failed to tap into the potential of prayer and nothing much has happened. The problem is we've not been taught how to pray successfully and we don't realise that it's more powerful than it appears to be. We don't know the secrets to prayer or the immeasurable benefits it can bring. We don't know what it actually means, because we've never properly tried to understand. Then one day we become so desperate for help that we drop down onto our knees and pray with everything we've got, and suddenly we realise that this 'prayer thing' actually works.

LET'S REINVENT IT

It's possible to reinvent what prayer means to us so that we can really begin to benefit from it. There are secrets to praying effectively which we're not normally made aware of, but if we were taught about the astonishing power within it, we would start to embrace it more. Instead of using it as a last resort, we would always go there first. Here are my 6 secrets to praying successfully, secrets I wish I'd known a long time ago.

NO 1:
UNANSWERED PRAYERS
'PRAYER FAILURE'

We've all had experiences of prayer failure which have given us 'proof' that prayer doesn't work, but the truth is, no prayer goes unanswered. The issue lies in our understanding and in what we're doing or not doing when we pray.

* We don't always believe that our prayers will be answered, so this immediately diminishes the power of our words. We ask, but we don't really expect to receive an answer, so our lack of belief hinders our results.

* We're not taught where the answers come from. We're not sure who or what answers them, so we miss the answers we're given. If we could understand that our prayers are answered in a myriad of ways that are both physical and non-physical - through songs, books, newspaper headlines, feelings, our intuition, and various other forms, we would become more attuned to the answers the more we practise.

* Maybe the problem is that we don't actually like the answer we've received, because we're being asked to change or to step up, and we're not sure we're good enough or ready for that yet, plus our frenetic nature means one day we're up for it and the next we're not.

* Maybe we're too scared to ask for a bigger life because we then have to deal with the responsibility that goes with it.

* We believe it's possible for a prayer to go unanswered, but no prayer actually goes unanswered. If we don't receive an answer, then that's an answer in itself. Sometimes we can miss the answer because we're looking for obvious, external changes, but the change can be as subtle as a small shift in our thoughts, feelings and perceptions.

WHAT'S BLOCKING OUR PRAYERS

If we feel we're experiencing 'prayer failure', we should always go within and ask if there are any blocks preventing our understanding, because there may be more that we need to know.

1. Too much control:

Our prayers aren't as effective when we're stressed and controlling, which is a habit we've learnt over time. The act of breathing for a few minutes each morning brings us back to a calmer perspective and relaxes our body, which is why there's an entire section on it in the Body Workout. When we allow our body to relax through breathing and our thoughts to settle through meditation, our emotions begin to settle too. We're in a more receptive state to tune into the universal power that's waiting to help us, instead of trying to control everything ourselves.

2. Disorder:

For our prayers to be effective we need to create order within ourselves and in our lives. This may mean releasing people, situations or habits that we no longer need, so we can create the time and reserve the energy to practise praying. Mentally, we might need to let go of certain beliefs and fears. In our hearts, we might need to let go of anger or resentment. Physically, we might need to clear out a room, car, desk or wardrobe. This inner and outer cleansing process makes space for all of our good to come to us because we're creating the space within ourselves and in our lives to accept it. The Universe likes order and responds to our efforts accordingly.

3. Holding onto grievances:

If our prayers are not being answered, we have to take an honest look inside of us to see if we're holding onto any grievances, as small as they may be, and ask to be shown how to release them. This frees us and other people and creates space in us and around us for our good to find us.

We can choose to hold onto a grievance, but if we do we'll just block our good. That's why there's a section dedicated to forgiveness in the Heart Workout, because of its immense liberating power.

4. Praying for a specific outcome (and why that doesn't work):

We generally pray for specific outcomes, which is why when we pray it doesn't always feel good, because it's more of a demand than a prayer. We should always ask in prayer for the highest good. Prayers can 'fail' when we're asking for what we think is the right outcome, but we don't always know what's best for us. Praying in this way is ineffective because it's limiting and the Universe won't support it. We're normally asking for material things like a baby, a partner, a new job, more money, or for a situation to be sorted in a particular way, or for a person to change so that we can be happy. But this is approaching prayer from the wrong perspective.

5. Our prayer may be too small:

A Course in Miracles says: **"You do not ask too much of life, but far too little."** (W-p1.133.2). Even though there's an abundance of good waiting for us, our power is limited by our thinking. The Universe cannot give us any greater blessing than we can believe is possible. We're taught to ask for a big and magnificent life, full of everything our heart desires. We're asked to come with an open mind and with no constricted ideas of what we think will make us happy.

We shouldn't apologise or be ashamed to ask for the highest good for ourselves and for the world. We should ask for an abundance of money so that we can use our energy to serve the world. We should ask for everything to unfold in the right way and at the right time, and to be shown the brilliance within us and in others too. We should ask to be used in a way that will make a difference to the world. That's when our prayers are taken seriously, and that's when they start to get answered in the most magnificent ways.

6. Lack of gratitude:

Giving thanks in advance for what we want to experience in our life is the fastest way to getting it, because we're coming from a mindset that believes we have it already. Saying thank you for all the success, abundance and joy in every area of our life is a much more effective prayer than saying: "I want more money" or just moaning that we feel unsuccessful By saying thank you in advance for the right outcome and the right understanding, or for being shown how to love well or being blessed with peace and happiness – that's when the Universe will respond and say: "Your wish is my command."

NO 2:
DELAYS

The Israelites weren't led along the shortest route to reach their Promised Land, they were taken the longest way on purpose. This seems extremely harsh and cruel and I'm sure they prayed just as we would have done to reach their destination as quickly as possible. Sometimes there's a delay in our prayers being answered for a reason. It might not look like anything is happening and maybe it's gone on for months, but we're asked to trust that work is going on behind the scenes for our highest good. The Bible tells us that the Israelites were actually being protected, because God knew they weren't prepared for war. By taking them on the longer route He was actually strengthening the army so that they would succeed in battle.

It's easy to say a prayer and think things aren't happening as quickly as we'd like, but that's where faith comes in. Faith isn't blind, and being faithful doesn't make us stupid. We'll always have faith in something, so we can either choose to have faith in the power of love to order our lives, or in the power of fear to cause chaos. Delays can seem annoying or frustrating, but they provide us with the opportunity to grow, to learn to let go and trust, or with the space for things to fall into place in a way that we could never have planned ourselves.

NO 3:
THE SECRETS TO SUCCESSFUL PRAYER

1. Consistency:

Prayer becomes powerful when we do it daily. It's better to pray sincerely for two minutes every morning than it is to have a long session once a week, become distracted and accomplish nothing. Being consistent makes it become a normal part of our daily routine. It becomes part of us and means we reconnect with it more quickly each time. A daily practice keeps us dwelling on the right frequency and within the right mindset. It allows us to stop for a few minutes every day and reconnect, actively tuning into our Higher Self and the wisdom that it wants us to hear.

2. Get down on your knees and join your hands:

I know this might feel weird, subservient and just not what you want to do, but honestly, it works. I'm not entirely sure why it works, but it does. It makes the practice so much more powerful. Perhaps it's because we're showing reverence to the power that can bring us all of the happiness and joy we're seeking. Think of it as a yoga pose or an anchor, because every time we get into the position we'll automatically feel more connected, and once we've closed our eyes we'll forget what position we're in anyway.

3. Pray out loud and internally:

The practice of prayer, either silently or out loud, has an explosive, vibratory power which can free us from life's difficulties and allow the limitations of our ego to be released. Internal prayer can be very powerful because it's directed straight to the heart, which can create intense feelings. but here's also something powerful about praying out loud, because of the effect it has on our vibration. I do both, depending on where I am and how I'm feeling. When we pray out loud it definitely has an uplifting, powerful effect, as long as you can get over the weird, embarrassing feelings, but no one's watching, and if they are, you'll soon be too happy to care.

4. Pray with all you've got:

Often when we pray there isn't much feeling behind it. If you've ever said the Lord's Prayer, most of the time we race through it, not paying much attention to the words. In order for our prayers to be effective, we have to pray with all we've got. Praying within us, rather than to something outside of us, means we're using more levels of our being, because we're connecting within. All aspects of our psyche are switched on. We start to feel the prayer throughout our body, we say the words passionately, we feel it in our hearts, our spirit is lifted, and our soul is awakened.

5. Find a prayer partner:

This turns up the effectiveness of prayer and takes it to another level. The Bible tells us: **"For where two or three are gathered together in My name, I am there in the midst of them."** (Matthew 18:20), which means where two or more are praying together for the highest good of all concerned, their prayers are powerful. There's generally more energy and more passion when we're with someone else, which helps us to feel it on every level, plus it stops us from just praying for ourselves.

6. Write them down:

Writing our prayers down allows us to focus on feeling the prayer instead of trying to remember what to say and how to say it. It means we can be more intentional and we'll be less likely to become lost in random thoughts and distractions.

NO4:
WHAT TO SAY (and what not to say)

Instead of asking for specific things, it never occurred to me to ask for guidance and wisdom. Nor did it occur to me to pray for strength instead of always asking for things to be easier. It never occurred to me to ask to be taught how to love well, or for my relationships to be restored, rather than just wishing people would change to suit me. It never occurred to me to ask to be shown the brilliance within me, instead of endlessly trying to fix the endless list of faults I thought I had. One request comes from a place of limitation and perceived lack, while the other comes from a belief in our unlimited potential.

INSTEAD OF SAYING:	WE COULD SAY:
"I want..."	"If it's for the highest good of everyone, may I have a promotion, a book deal, a new career, more success?"

INSTEAD OF SAYING:	WE COULD SAY:
"It doesn't seem fair, why isn't this situation being sorted?"	"Help me to understand what's going on. What do I need to do or stop doing? What do I need to learn? Help me to become stronger, not for things to be easier."
"I don't know what to do about...or I don't know why it's happening."	"Show me the truth about this situation..."
"I don't know what to do with my career/my life."	"Lift my thoughts - use my voice, my talents, my skills and my passions in a way that would serve the world."
"I wish they'd change."	"Show me how to love well and see the good in others."
I wish .... would happen."	"To be honest, I'm not exactly sure what I want or what the best outcome is, but I'm willing to be guided instead. Instead of me thinking I know what's best, I'm going to trust."

INSTEAD OF SAYING:	WE COULD SAY:
"I want more money."	"Thank you for blessing me with an abundance of money so I can focus on making a difference in the world."
"I want to be free from fear."	"Thank you for releasing me from the conditions of mind which created the fear."
"Make this suffering go away."	"Please use my mind to transform this experience. Please transform my perception of the experience, transform the situation, and transform me. Thank you for sending me a miracle."

INSTEAD OF SAYING:	WE COULD SAY:
"I want<fill in the blank>) A baby for example."	"I'd love a baby of my own. I trust that if it's right for me to be a mother it will happen at the right time and in the right way. For now though, I'm going to forget about it, go and have some fun, and trust that I'm being looked after."

NO 5:
THE HIGHEST PRAYERS

PRAYER NO 1: SURRENDER

There is a prayer from *A Course in Miracles* which is a complete surrendering to the notion that we don't exactly know what we want or how to make everything happen, but we're willing to be guided instead. This means we're opening our minds, freeing ourselves from limitation, and opening the way up for our highest good to be released. The prayer is:

> What would You have me do?
> Where would You have me go?
> What would You have me say, and to who?
> (W-p1.71.9:2)

Where it says in the Bible: *"Your will be done"* (Matthew 6:10), it means we're not sure what would make us happy, but we're willing to be shown. We've tried to manifest what we think we want and we're still not completely satisfied. We know we're not showing up like we could be, but we're not exactly sure what to do. We've tried for long enough now to fix ourselves to still feel like we have work to do. This prayer is a clear statement that we're willing to be guided instead.

PRAYER NO 2:
AN INSIDE JOB

The most powerful prayer we can ask is that we become the person we would need to be in order to have what we desire. This means we're asking to be changed from the inside out. We need to ask to be shown, to be guided. If you want to be successful in business, imagine how you would walk, talk, think, act and feel? If you want to be promoted, to become a mother, or to change careers, who would you need to be to become that person? What would you have to stop doing? What would you have to *start* doing? We have to be on the same frequency as the thing we desire. We can't desire more when we're living in a limited mindset. The prayer could sound like this:

"Help me to become the person I would need to be to have ....." or "Make me the wife, mother, daughter, sister, colleague, businesswoman, entrepreneur, neighbour and friend that you would have me be so I can do what you want me to do."

I used to want a sexy career and I was embarrassed to tell people what I did. Surely I was meant to do more than work in a dull, corporate office, but I wasn't rising to the occasion. I would turn up at work ungrateful, negative and complaining, knowing I was only there for the money. I needed to understand this about myself to help me become the person I knew I was capable of being before I could expect a new career to land on my lap. A new job wasn't the answer - the same 'me' would show up at any company. I had to ask to be changed on the inside first.

It's always an inside job.

By asking this divine intelligence and wisdom within us for help - we'll be shown all the places within us that we need to look at to enable us to move forward. It can seem like things are getting worse because we'll be shown aspects of our personality that aren't too appealing, but it's a clearing-up process, and it's a process which removes any blocks to us receiving all the good that's been waiting for us.

NO 6:
HOW ARE PRAYERS ANSWERED?

An answered prayer is very personal. People talk about coincidences, but when you've asked for help and received it, you know. It's so personal that other people won't understand it, and that's fine. It doesn't always come via a megaphone telling the world what's happened. A miracle is a shift in how we think and perceive, so it's not always evident to others what's going on within the depths of our heart and mind. Nothing appears to have changed on the outside, but inside our minds and our thoughts may be lifted and our fears are transcended. To the world, nothing has happened, but inside of us there's a shift. Maybe it was just that we lightened up and started to see the good in someone instead of perceiving their faults. Or maybe we began to think more positively, and this has completely changed how our day has worked out.

We think our prayers are only answered by something outside of us which we don't understand, so we think they've gone unanswered. We don't realise that other people can also answer our prayers, but this only works if we let them. Our faith in others is matched by our faith in ourselves. If we just concentrate on how much they annoy us, or we see them as not good enough, then we won't be able to hear the message they have for us. If we choose to see the good in them instead, we'll be able to hear what they are trying to tell us.

Our prayers might be answered by a comment someone makes, by a book they've written, or in a workshop they're holding. It might be in a song lyric, an email or a news article. There are an infinite number of ways that our prayers can be answered. The secret is to tune in every day and allow ourselves to be divinely guided. The guidance may not come from where we expect it to come from - it might come from a stranger we're about to meet, or through someone we've forgiven. I've been surprised many times to find the answer can be found in the most unexpected people and places.

When we're praying, we tune in. Once we've said a prayer our vibration is lifted and we need to become more aware to receive the response and listen to our internal wisdom, which we can hear when we become quiet.

NO 7:
HOW TO HEAR OUR INNER GUIDE

Up to now you've relaxed your body through breathing and you've created space in your heart through forgiveness. Once you've said your prayers, you can begin to connect with this wisdom through meditation, because you'll be dwelling within the deepest part of your mind - your superconscious mind. Because you've chosen to be still and you've created some quiet time away from the world's noise and distractions, now you have the opportunity to hear your own internal wisdom and allow it to guide you.

After spending years following my own advice, asking other people for theirs and getting it wrong, I was determined to learn how to be guided instead. It took a while for me to learn this and even longer to trust in it. So here's my guide to help you hear your own internal teacher and the guidance within you. This really is the most amazing part of going within because you'll be able to access the wisdom within you whenever you need it and you'll wonder how you ever lived without it.

STEP 1:
ASK

This is our opportunity to pray and to ask for any guidance we need or for anything we desire. When we have a dilemma or a decision to make, we tend to go around asking everyone we know for advice and by the end of it we're still none the wiser. Instead we should always remember to go within and direct our requests within us.

STEP 2:
LISTEN

When we meditate we have the opportunity to become still and quiet. Because we've prayed, we have the opportunity to hear our own internal teacher, our inner guide, and the wisdom it wants us to hear. It's an opportunity for our soul to speak to us. This seems like a strange concept at first, but it's actually incredibly natural – we've just forgotten it exists and we're unpractised at connecting with it. And as we reconnect, we start to live in a different world.

I had a client who had an issue at work which was creating a lot of stress and uncertainty. He felt overwhelmed, anxious and at times quite depressed, but he learned how to ask for guidance instead of getting lost in the craziness. His exact question was: "Is this (situation) going to turn out ok?" And the calm response he received back was: "Yes, it'll take another two weeks, but it'll be fine."

The voice he heard was subtle, it didn't scream at him. It was a deep sense, a feeling, a calm voice of strength and wisdom within his mind. Even though he was practised at asking and listening, he still doubted the answer, and often slipped into worrying about the outcome. The majority of the time he felt a sense of peace, which is hard to understand until you've experienced it. Whenever he felt agitated, he asked again for help: "Is this situation going to be ok?" And each time he received a calm feeling and the same response: "Yes, it's all fine."

Our prayers are answered in a variety of ways and everyone has different experiences. If we've prayed for strength, someone may become available to help us out. If we've prayed for more love, a book may land at our feet to help us. If we've prayed for more joy, a new hobby might appear on our radar. If we've asked for guidance, a newspaper headline might grab our attention. And once we've prayed and asked, we learn to listen and to remember to be aware to receive the answer, trusting that it's on its way.

(And if you're wondering, the stressful situation my client was in turned out completely fine and worked out even better than he imagined. And it did take two weeks longer, just like he'd been guided.)

FAQ'S :-)
WHERE IS MY INTERNAL TEACHER?

It's right inside of us. It's our soul speaking to us, our Higher Self guiding us. It's the inner wisdom and the Truth that we have the opportunity to connect with and hear every single day.

I'M NOT SURE I CAN HEAR IT

If we can't hear it, it's just because we're unpractised at listening. The voice of our internal teacher within us is called the still, small voice of God and it speaks of love and peace, but the loud voice of our ego gets in there first and drowns it out. This voice will never compete with our ego and it will never scream and shout at us like the ego does with its erratic demands. It will simply guide us, quietly and consistently. It's always been guiding us, we've just not been tuned in to it. No matter how many detours we've taken, or how many mistakes we think we've made, no matter what we've been through or experienced, it's always nudging us back on track.

WHAT DOES IT SOUND LIKE?

I used to think I couldn't hear my internal guidance because the only voices in my head were mine. One voice seemed to scream at me all day long - telling me I wasn't enough, or telling what was wrong, or what might go wrong. It spoke of hate and limitation. The other voice spoke to me in meditation, and it told me the opposite.

In time I realised both voices were mine. One voice was my ego - the mindset I was in when I was needy, grasping, controlling and coming from a place of fear. The other voice was still me, but it was coming from my Higher Self - the mindset I was in when I was trusting, grateful, filled with joy and love, and coming from a place of peace and complete security. Both voices inside our minds are ours and both have completely different messages for us and, ultimately, completely opposing results. It's up to us which voice we choose to listen to.

IS IT A VOICE OR A FEELING?

It can be one or the other, or both. When we're meditating, we can listen for the still, small voice of our internal teacher that's always guiding us. This divine intelligence within us will tell us everything we need to know. This voice is the highest, most loving thought we have and the clearest word. It's also experienced as a subtle feeling which goes unrecognised because we're not always aware.

SERIOUSLY, I'M CONFUSED BY THE MESSAGES I'M RECEIVING

If we're confused by any guidance or sign we've received, it's because we're listening to two voices instead of one. Because we're more accustomed to our ego and less used to meditating, our ego seems to control us and it seems to be the only voice we hear. Our Higher Self won't compete with this, but it won't abandon us either. It'll wait patiently for us to connect to it so that we can hear the guidance it's been trying to give us all along. Gradually, the answers become so clear and precise, there's no doubt that they're correct.

When we're tempted to listen to the wrong voice, it's usually because we're coming from a place of fear and impatience. If we want to make progress now and we haven't received an answer yet, our ego will prompt us to take action, even if it's not for our highest good. In this situation, we're told to ask for help and understanding. If we haven't received an answer, it doesn't mean one isn't on its way.

Some spiritual teachers tell us that when we receive an answer to our question from the voice within we'll feel at peace. When we're new to accessing this guidance we're not always sure which voice has directed us, and if we're not meditating regularly it's more likely that our ego is running the show. And in time, we'll learn which voice is guiding us by how we feel.

From experience, the right answer comes from the calmest voice within us. It's us when we're at our most confident, peaceful and sure of ourselves. If the guidance we receive sounds crazy, reckless and downright wrong, and if it goes against what our conscious mind (and everyone else) is telling us to do, it doesn't mean it's incorrect.

HOW DO I HEAR THIS GUIDANCE MORE OFTEN BECAUSE I KEEP MAKING THE WRONG DECISIONS?

The purpose of this chapter is to help us access our internal teacher every day. It's possible to hear only one voice, but this depends on which mindset we choose to live within and what we choose to believe. We can't just meditate and expect to be an enlightened master all day long. We have to keep bringing ourselves back to the remembrance of the Truth about ourselves at regular intervals.

It sounds like hard work, but the return on investment is astounding. It actually saves us time in the end, because we're not wasting effort on the wrong things and we're being guided towards what's right instead. It begins to take less effort the more we do it. It takes practice to hear our internal wisdom, and willingness to learn what it sounds like, but it's definitely worth the effort because it takes the responsibility and pressure off us to work everything out for ourselves.

STEP 3:
TRUST

Don't be concerned if this doesn't happen overnight. Our guidance often comes to us in direct proportion to our ability to completely surrender. When we can let go and be open to the prospect of infinite possibility, then we're opening ourselves up for a miracle.

SPIRIT: SUMMARY

* The power of prayer is phenomenal. The highest prayers are when we surrender our desires and release our attachment to particular outcomes. When we ask for ourselves to change and we pray for others, that's when we see amazing results

* Believe your prayers will be answered. Direct your prayers within you. Pray with feeling, energy and passion. And do it daily. Become aware of how your prayers are answered. Trust and have patience, because if you don't get an immediate answer it doesn't mean the prayer has failed

* Always ask for the highest good. Ask big. Take off the limits. Ask for a big life, but also ask to be changed on the inside to match it. Prayer can blow our minds, overcome limitations and take us to a new level.

Now you've done all of the inner work, it's time to let your soul speak to you.

Which is exactly where we're going next...

This is the perfect final piece of the jigsaw, because if we've been following the exercises so far then our soul is becoming louder and ever more persistent. This is the deep work when we work from the inside-out. It's why the mindset work alone doesn't work as powerfully if all other parts of our psyche aren't aligned. Through embracing the last 4 chapters, we're taking off the limits. We're reconnecting all parts of us so we're working together now, for our Highest Good.

- We've taken ourselves out of fight or flight

- We've accessed a deeper part of our mind

- We've removed the blocks surrounding our hearts

- And we've taken off the limits through uplifting our spirit, our vibe, our disposition, our attitude.

And this is where our power is. This is where all of the work we've been doing starts to pay off.

MISSING PIECE NO 4
YOUR **SOUL**

***

Our soul is speaking to us every day, asking us to rise up and become the person we're capable of being. There's a divine plan laid out for our lives - a purpose we're here for and a mission we've been sent here to complete. When we do the work in this book, we're being healed so that we can release the old thought patterns and beliefs which are no longer aligned to the frequency of our souls. Sometimes we know what we need to release, other times we have no idea, we just constantly feel blocked, and this is why the work we need to do is **More Than A Mindset.** (I know I keep saying this but it's true because our minds don't always know the answers.) And with everything's that''s going on in the world right now, there's never been a more important time for us all to step up.

So far we've worked to realign our body, mind, heart and spirit to enable our soul to awaken. This begins to create a sense of great inner peace, harmony and inner strength that we'll see reflected in our outer world. The battle for self-mastery continues, but we find it becomes less tumultuous because we're gradually feeling more grounded. We can begin to hear our own inner wisdom now we're out of the craziness of fight or flight and the constant noise and distractions. And we find life becomes easier to navigate because if our decisions are not in harmony with our new values, we immediately have our answer.

Remembering that we live from the inside-out means we can access a place of perfect peace and complete security whenever we desire, because it's all within us. Everything we've been searching for is within us - we've just disconnected for a while whilst we looked outside of ourselves for the answer to our misery, seeking success and approval from the world around us. Now we're remembering that we're more than we appear to be and we're becoming ever more willing to be guided exclusively by our soul.

We've wasted precious mental energy trying to find ourselves, to understand what our purpose is, or to decide what career we should be in. We've wasted precious mental energy trying to change the effects, instead of working on the cause. And we've engaged in an intense battle to overcome ourselves and everything we thought was wrong with us. Until now!

THE WORLD'S DEFINITION OF SUCCESS

The world has a definition of success that we've unknowingly bought into which tells us every day whether we're successful or not, based on its disordered demands. We've felt empty, lost and confused whilst chasing its turbulent goals. At times we've felt like a failure and at times we've felt judged. At times we've felt like we're falling behind because we're assessed on how successful we are based on the car we drive, the money we earn and the house we live in.

And there's certainly nothing wrong with having these things. In fact, the Bible encourages us to prosper: **"I pray that you may prosper in all things and be in health, just as your soul prospers."** (3 John 2.)

It's wonderful to have these things, but surely only if we feel fulfilled at the same time. And that depends on how they're being paid for in terms of what our soul is doing (or more importantly, not doing). There are times when underneath the surface of perfection and belongings lie deeply unhappy people.

This chaotic definition of success seems normal to us, until we begin to awaken to the idea that's it's keeping us down. The world needs us to step up, but we're too focused on what we can do and buy to make us feel successful, because that masks the emptiness we feel inside and helps us to hide in the background. We've been chained to an endless rhythm where nothing is ever enough, yet the world suffers more because we're not releasing our gifts.

But we're starting to sense that this isn't working for us anymore. We're starting to wonder what our world might look like if we created a new definition of success where we followed our dreams instead, even when the doubting voice in our head is screaming at us to stay where we are. Even when we're not exactly sure what we want to do, because we have a sense we have more to give. We're starting to wonder what our life might look like when we're focusing on uplifting the world rather than just focusing on what we can get from it.

OUR PERSONAL DEFINITION OF SUCCESS

If our head hits the pillow each night and we feel contented because we've managed to drag ourselves through another day working in a job we don't love, but we feel successful because it pays for the new cars, the house and the lifestyle. If we're ignoring that stirring in our soul to do something we love – something that would make a difference and allow us to release our greatness, but we put off what it's asking us to do for another day, or until we retire. Is this living? Is this success?

If our head hits the pillow each night and we feel contented because we've happily spent the day working on our destiny – perhaps on a mission to create a business or a brand that will make a difference. We don't have a contract promising us what the rewards will be (yet), we haven't upgraded our cars or bought that big house, but we're following what we're being guided to do. Even though it feels scary and downright crazy at times. Maybe we haven't got the prizes yet and we're wondering if they'll ever come. Is this living? Is this success?

If we're happy in either scenario, then you could argue that we're successful. If we're unhappy in either scenario, then you could argue that we're not. Notice the difference between the two: scenario one comes from a "What can I get?" mentality - in other words: "What can I earn and how can I earn it to provide and maintain my lifestyle." Scenario two comes from a giving mentality, where we understand that there's a mission we're working on that can help to serve people and uplift the world - a mission, as the Bhagavad Gita explains, where we're detached from the results, because we simply can't ignore our soul anymore. And when we approach life in this way suddenly all the rewards we've been chasing land at our feet, thanks to our new non-resistant consciousness.

There's a third scenario though which falls somewhere between these two. In this scenario, we're no longer attached to what we can get, but equally we're not yet doing anything worthwhile that feeds our soul. We're gathering strength to step out of conformity but we're stuck in between these two worlds, complaining about what's wrong with our lives and not knowing what to do with them.

If our core belief is that we're unsuccessful, nothing we can do or buy can heal this belief. That feeling of inadequacy can creep back to the surface within an hour of us buying that next thing we think we desperately need. No one can make us feel like a failure unless we allow them to. People simply project their own definition of success on us and if we're not strong enough, we'll automatically compare ourselves against it. It's a dangerous place to be when we're living by someone else's rules. We expose ourselves to so much suffering when we don't have enough clarity around our own values and our own version of success.

The lure of possessions is often too tempting. We want everything right now so we'll feel successful, even if it means getting into debt or ignoring our soul in the process.

Just because the world is set up this way, it doesn't mean we need to follow that path. We're in a position where we can create our own definition of success, regardless of how different it appears to be.

Once we start to become less attached to what we can get and more open to how we can serve the world, we're beginning to listen to our soul. This means the spark of divinity with us has been ignited and it won't go away, however much we try to resist it. Even if we're not aware it's lit, or we ignore it, doubt or actively resist it, it will keep nudging us until we finally do something about it. If you're thinking: "This all sounds lovely but I need my job to pay for everything!" It doesn't mean we need to quit our jobs all of a sudden if we have responsibilities to meet. It does mean though that we can at least make a start, even if it's at the side of our desks.

SO FREAKED OUT BY OUR POTENTIAL

Our soul is always nudging us but there's something in the way. It's that 4 letter word we've talked about before. The more we do the work in this book, the less impact these 4 letters will have over us. It's called FEAR but not as we know it. We fear listening to our soul because:

- We might discover we are more than anyone ever thought we could be, even those closest to us

- We might possess the talent we sensed in our hearts we had within us

- We might just discover how we're a little more powerful, loveable and stronger than we've previously thought

- We might just possess enough courage to actually make a start (finally!)

- We fear that we've actually correctly interpreted the guidance we've received in terms of what our soul has been nudging us to do

- We fear that if we start to embrace our Higher Self, we'll have to show we're worthy of living this way, and that freaks us out more than anything.

F-E-A-R

It's fear that keeps us trapped in jobs we don't love because we don't believe in ourselves or the Universe enough to imagine there's another way. We worry about how we're going to survive and whether people will buy our products, or need our services. We worry we'll be ridiculed, or accused of being selfish for being unconventional and following our dreams. We fear the unknown and being alone, and we're scared it won't work out. We're trapped in an intense battle for self-mastery between the fears we've become lost in and the potential we try to deny.

We've wasted precious time chasing goals and possessions because they're seen as the epitome of success, but now we're beginning to ask ourselves deeper questions. We've looked to other people to tell us we're good enough, forgetting we're good enough already. We've fitted into society's mould, we've stayed within the confines of our ego's limited mindset, and we've ignored the calling of our soul.

Except this time we can't ignore it.

THINK AGAIN

We've been taught for thousands of years that we don't need to conform to the world and we've also been taught how to attain our freedom:

"And do not be conformed to this world, but be transformed by the renewing of your mind."
(Romans 12:2)

Renewing our mind means thinking outside the box, listening to our soul's guidance, and following our dreams. Imagining a job that makes our soul come alive whilst earning a decent salary doesn't require a degree or letters after our name; but it does require courage and faith.

The wisest teachers we've been blessed with have always encouraged us to run our own race, to create a vision of what success means to us, and to have the tenacity and focus to keep working towards that, no matter how many distractions tempt us away and no matter who doesn't support us or tries to keep us down. The world teaches us that we'll be successful if we own certain possessions, but our soul reminds us that we're already more than enough and encourages us to just make a start.

SO HOW DO WE CHANGE?

OUR REAL PURPOSE

Our purpose in life seems to revolve around our careers, where we work, and what our job title is. When we become dispirited in our careers, we begin a wider search for meaning. We think: "Surely we were sent here to do more than this!"

Whilst on one hand we do find purpose through work, we also have an internal, spiritual purpose of self-mastery. We think they're two separate things, when in fact they're more closely linked than we can imagine. The problem is, we usually get those two priorities the wrong way round and spend our days agonising over and focusing on our careers.

Our purpose in life isn't something we need to go out and find, manufacture or stress over. It's right in front of us. And once we've overcome our resistance to embracing it, our worldly career naturally falls into place. In Buddhism, we're told that our purpose in life is to overcome Dukkha, which is the mental suffering we experience through our personal thoughts, feelings and emotions. This is our intimate battle for self-mastery, a battle between the person we're being, versus the person we want to be. We expect to get a new career first and then we'll start to show up, but it actually works the other way round.

Our main purpose in life is to download love every day and to live it - where our thoughts are high and the good we want for ourselves is something we also want for everyone else too. It's a place where no one is better than us - even if they have more money or more fame – and no one is less than us, no matter where they live or which car they drive. By living like this we're being our Higher Self. We're actually practising the theory we're learning about. We're not just trying to change our mindset, we're actually living and breathing it.

What would people think of us if we started releasing the best that's within us? Would they still like us? And what if we started to be happy and positive? Wouldn't we piss people off? Maybe. As we begin to focus our efforts on showing up, our life realigns itself to match the higher version of ourselves that we're expressing. Instead of focusing on the money or the job title, we'll either begin to appreciate and show up fully in our current career, or we'll be guided elsewhere. Other people will then follow our lead because they'll begin to recognise their own potential too.

**"Seek ye first the Kingdom of God,
and all things shall be added unto you."**
(Matthew 6:33)

Means:

Adopt an attitude of love, fill your heart with love and everything you've dreamed of will come to you.

We've been taught: "Put no other gods before me." (Exodus 20:3). This isn't God being controlling and telling us we should only believe in Him because He's scared we'll find what we're looking for in someone else and he'll end up with fewer followers. He's telling us not to put any other goals before love. But we do. We choose jobs and careers purely for the money.

The truth is, we're afraid to put love first, because we might just find more love within ourselves and within other people than we've ever experienced before. Seeking the Kingdom of God and aiming for Heaven on Earth means we're seeking to dwell in a space where love is the foundation. It's asking us to let go of our attachment to results and to aim for love as the highest feeling and experience throughout our lives so that we make all of our decisions from this more enlightened mindset. And we're promised that when we do this, we'll receive everything we've always wanted.

If all this love, God, Heaven and enlightenment work sounds too hippy or fluffy to make a significant difference, it's up to us what we choose to believe. How much more pain do we want to keep experiencing before we give love a real go?

OUR EGO'S LIMITING DREAM

Our ego's dreams sound like this: "I want to earn more money so that I can buy a new house because then I'll feel good enough." It tells us we'll be happy once we've changed careers, met someone special, once we have more savings, earn more money, or drive a new car. Our ego wants everything now. It's like an instant cup of coffee. It's blocked our dreams and silenced our souls. It's either lamenting over the past or anxious over the future. Our ego represents chaos, fear and limitation.

OUR SOUL'S LIMITLESS DREAM

The dream within our soul is wise and deep and speaks of what we can give, not what we can get. In the Bible it's described as the burning bush. It represents the still, small voice of God, the voice of love within us, our soul, our Higher Self which is guiding us constantly to step up, to follow our dreams, to rise to the occasion, to make a difference, and to change our priorities. And this burning bush, this constant nudge to grow won't ever go away. Once the spark has been lit, that's it, it never goes out.

HOW TO TURN OUR LIVES AROUND

Too often we focus on what's wrong in our lives: "My job is so depressing and boring / I want a more fulfilling career / more money / a nicer boss / a bigger house / a new partner / to be free from fear."

The Universe is bored of listening to our complaints. We're making our problems bigger, we're making them our gods, and then we wonder why nothing changes. We're not trusting and believing because things have been this way for years, so why would they suddenly change now.

What if we said instead: "Ok Universe, you've placed this dream in my heart but I've no idea how it will ever happen. I know you know the right people and you can open the right doors for me at the right time, and I know that with you, all things are possible."

Or we could say: "Ok Universe, I'm so unhappy in my current work, it doesn't light up my soul and I don't enjoy it, but it pays the bills. I don't exactly know what to believe in, but I'm kind of fed up trying to work everything out for myself so I'm going to start trusting that the skills I have can be used in a way to serve the world. I don't know how or when, but I'm going to have a little patience and trust you will tell me what I need to know."

And the Universe is like - finally, let's get moving! We're making our doubt and problems smaller. That's when we're trusting. That's when the power of the love within us can begin to work miracles.

WE'RE ALWAYS BELIEVING

It all comes down to belief. Do we have faith in the promise that however small our circumstances may appear to be, the power working within us can take us further than we can imagine? Do we realise we have the world's power and strength within us? Or do we have more faith in lack, limitation, fear and doubt? Do we believe our requests might not be received, our desires won't matcrialise, and that this power is nonsense?

We're experts at asking: "I want a new car / new job / new partner / more money / more happiness / more fulfilment." We're not so good at believing the promises of inner peace, health, abundance and joy, so we don't receive all that we're entitled to and we think it doesn't work, that the promises are false, and that this power doesn't exist.

If there's something we desire that isn't happening for us, then it's not the Universe who's blocking our good, it's us. Could we really be afraid of having what we desire? Who would we need to be? How would we need to show up? What sort of responsibilities would we have to step up to? What personality characteristics would we have to start owning? If our desire is to start our own business, enter into a new career, or receive a promotion, what would we have to start (or stop) doing? Are we ready to step into our greatness? Will people still like us? Will they try to silence us or mock us? Are we ready for that?

WHEN WE'RE NOT SUPPORTED
(and why)

I spoke to one of my clients, Kylie in Australia (not Kylie Minogue!) and she told me how when she was opening her yoga studio, the people closest to her didn't back her and she felt let down. Other yogi friends and friends in her community told her it wouldn't work because people wouldn't connect with her style of yoga. Her father never asked her how it was going and she felt like he didn't care.

We're often surprised when support doesn't come from the people closest to us. They doubt us, mock us or think we're just dreaming, and it happens all the time.

People who haven't had the courage to step into their own greatness – people who gave up on a dream or didn't even give it a try, or who allowed their own fears to overwhelm them – often voice their own internal doubts and fears at us. And if we're not strong enough, it can knock our confidence. One defeatist remark is enough to stop us in our tracks.

As Kylie spoke, she was obviously too passionate about her dream to stop, because she was on a mission. She had reached a place where she could feel compassion towards those who doubted her because she understood that their doubts stemmed from their own personal fears. Kylie's bravery was showing them what could be done, and – by contrast - what they were failing to do. The resistance she was encountering was because she was shining her light and highlighting to those close to her what was actually possible.

STEPPING OUT, RISING UP

Life is tough at times when you don't fit the mould. We're not always aware that we can create our own rules. We're not celebrated for being different. People are confused if we don't follow the norm because we're going against what society is telling us to do. We're being brave and we're doing what other people only ever hope to do. Some people think we're stupid or crazy. And sometimes we believe them. Thankfully sometimes we don't.

The prospect of reaching the end of your life without giving your dreams a chance - is that not enough of a motivator? What if taking the safe route would be, in your opinion, a slow death, whereas having the courage to follow a dream might be terrifying and completely unknown, but you know you're doing what you were put here to do. Would you feel alive, excited, passionate and also scared, doubtful, lost and confused - of course!

When you can't work in a corporate environment anymore, you don't want a difficult boss breathing down your neck, and the money doesn't motivate you enough to devote one more day to a job that doesn't light up your soul, something is motivating you to change.

Maybe you've taken the risk to work for yourself and it's taken longer than you thought to see the rewards of your efforts. You've experienced some tough times and people are questioning your efforts, but something still drives you on.

Maybe you have a dream in your heart and a vision of your future, but you have absolutely no idea how it will manifest and when. You don't feel good enough at times, you don't have the right network or contacts to push your idea forward. You feel like you're falling behind and you'll never achieve your dreams, but something still drives you on.

"With God All Things Are Possible."
(Luke 18:24-43)

Which means:
"With Love Everything Is Possible."

It's possible to reach a point where we have the courage to believe in ourselves, even if no one is backing us. And actually, if people are unconsciously stopping us from rising up or are not actively supporting us, then we can use it as a signal to know we must be onto something great.

It's up to us what we choose to focus on. If we believe *their* fears, we'll stop. If we believe the Truth, we'll continue. The more we're scared of our calling, the more we have to do it. If we're paralysed by fear, all we have to do is make a start.

WHAT IFS

What if...you have no idea what to do.

You're in a job or career you don't particularly like and don't want to stay in. You can't imagine spending another year in the role but you don't know what else to do. When some advice tells you to follow your passion and do what you love, and other advice tells you not to, it can be hard to know what to do. Here are some powerful questions to ask yourself:

- What sets your soul on fire?

- What do you love doing?

- What would you do even if you weren't paid for doing it?

- What are you doing when you lose track of time?

- What do you love learning about?

- What are you passionate about?

- What frustrates you or annoys you that you'd like to change?

- What kind of issues have you faced and overcome and could your transformation help others?

- What are you complimented on most?

- What do others look to you for?

- What do you have the most fun doing?

- What makes you feel great about yourself?

- What are you naturally good at?

- What do you most often give to others?

- What ideas, things, places and people are you most inspired by?

After answering these questions, what pattern do you see?

What if...you know what you want to do but...

You're frightened and freaked out by the prospect of starting (whether you've admitted it to yourself or not). You're scared of being 'new', having no followers, having no promise of success, not knowing where to start. You're concerned about what people will think.

Are you scared you're not ready or that you're not good enough? Are thoughts of "Who am I?" overwhelming you? Is self-doubt screaming at you? Then as my coach said:" Lean in and start. Just make a start however small. Trust that it's only fear and it'll start to have less control over you when you start."

What if...you just don't know what your purpose is?

Are you sure you don't know now you know nothing is impossible? Your fear of inadequacy has been acknowledged and you're starting to develop an unshakeable belief in yourself, because you're becoming aware of the power that dwells within you. You're becoming aware you are greater than you know, stronger than you've ever realised, and that you're constantly supported and being guided at every moment.

If you had all the confidence in the world and nothing was stopping you, what would you do differently?

What if...you've tried a new career but it didn't work out.

Did you try hard enough? Did you really give it a go? Did you really step in and fill the shoes of the person you wanted to be? Did fear get in the way? Did you try and realise it wasn't for you? Then that's not a bad thing because it's guiding you elsewhere.

What if... you really don't know, plus you feel you can't make a move right now because of circumstances and everything that's going on in the world: you have bills to pay and children to feed?

Then the best thing to do is to show up with everything you've got, right where you are. Because who is most likely to be kept on, promoted and find new doors opening for them because of their attitude? When we show up wherever we are, the Universe responds. Following our passion doesn't mean we need to quit our jobs straight away. We can transition into our passion over time. Some people say we don't need passion for what we do, others say it's key. Personally, after a lot of debating and asking the most successful people for their opinion on this, I agree with the majority that it's key. Passion is what comes from your soul and when your soul is alive and turned on, our life works in the most magnificent ways.

SOUL: EXERCISE

Through all of the work we've done so far, our souls are awakening naturally and will continue to do so. The more we let go and allow our lives to unfold, the more we'll live in complete alignment with the natural order of the Universe. The secret to manifesting a life we love isn't to visualise what we're typically taught to visualise. Instead of focusing on our dreams and our goals and forcing them through into our experience, the secret is two fold:

1. Instead of visualising the perfect job, more money or a new partner, whatever it is we want, the secret is to visualise and feel what these things would feel like when we have them. How would we feel if we loved our work, if we lived with passion, if our souls felt alive everyday? How would that feel? We've got to intensify the feeling because that's what makes it appear real right now. Plus it instantly shifts our energy state from being bored, unexcited, depressed, weak, lost, confused, guilty, or any other negative feeling that's going on inside of us. Instead of trying to force our way out of how we're feeling, we're just asked to do one small thing to lift our vibe. It might be a hot bath with candles, it might be a run, it might be to meditate, or dance to our favourite music. The barrier lies in thinking we have to force our way out of feelings, or overcome them, the secret lies in us creating a small shift in our energy.

2. The second secret is to imagine who we would have to *be* to live in alignment with our desires and attract them to us. How would we show up, how would we walk, talk, think,

speak and act? There's usually a significant difference in the way we would show up and how we're showing up now. The more we do the work in this book, the more we have no choice but to show up in a different way.

SOUL: SUMMARY

* Create your own definition of success. Live in line with your values and every decision you need to make will become much easier, because you'll have an immediate answer if it doesn't align with your soul. If you don't know what your values are, think about what's most important to you.

* Take off the limits. Focus on what you can give, not just what you can get, so you can begin to make a difference. When you feel fear and people don't support you, continue taking action, however small a step it seems and however much self-doubt is in your way.

* Our real purpose is to show up every day and to be our Higher Self. Our soul reminds us daily that we're already enough and we have the potential to achieve our dreams, if we're willing to open ourselves up to the messages. By showing up in life we'll start to change our energy, and in turn our experiences and the opportunities that become available to us will change too.

Now we'll move onto Part 2 of the book called: The Experience. This is the part where we can learn how to be the person we are meant to be on a daily basis.

The theory is great, but it's the experience we're really after.

PART 2:
THE EXPERIENCE

THE **EXPERIENCE**
INTRODUCTION

Here we are, the place where all of the practices we've looked at so far are together, so it's easy for us to refer back to.

A POWERFUL PRESCRIPTION

What's in The Experience is a powerful prescription. It's enough to put many doctors, psychiatrists and pharmaceutical companies out of business. And the best bit? All of this is available to us every day, with no monthly subscription. We could continue to create endless vision boards and ask for what we want, but if we don't do the work from the inside-out then it remains a very tiring process.

WHY DO WE WORK FROM THE INSIDE-OUT?

The Experience has taken years of work to research, create and refine. There have been many hours spent practising techniques that had little impact. Through sheer determination I've been able to fine-tune these practices which I've found make the most profound difference. It's a complete transformation for our entire being, both physical and non-physical and from the inside out. This means we're able to heal on every level. The inside is what's happening within - in the thoughts we hold in our minds and the feelings we cherish within our hearts. The outside is the experience of our life, which is felt through the health of our body, the vibrancy of our spirit and in the happiness of our soul.

If we're holding on to the belief that we're not good enough, however well disguised it is, then every area of our life aligns itself to this belief. It begins as an unrecognised thought or feeling then gradually morphs into who we are. The problem isn't that we don't have the secrets to success. The problem is that we're avoiding doing the work, because we struggle to overcome the barrage of resistance we encounter on a daily basis. Instead, we buy into what our ego tells us we are and we let it beat us down.

CREATE SPACE:
MENTALLY

We need to make space for this new morning routine in our lives, both mentally and physically. Often this means we need to be more mindful about how we spend our days. Who are we spending them with? Do we need to release people, situations or circumstances that are no longer serving us? What are we spending our time on? Where is our energy going? Are we spending our days living in line with our values? What do we need to start doing, and what do we need to stop doing?

It's easier to sit and watch TV than it is to sit down and meditate because working on ourselves requires more effort. Meditation *is* work, but it becomes non-negotiable when we understand its benefits and start to feel them. In fact, we begin to wonder how we ever lived without it.

CREATE SPACE:
PHYSICALLY

Our physical environment doesn't need to be fancy, but it does need to be something we can recreate wherever we go. All we need is a simple meditation cushion (a pillow or cushion works fine too) and a mobile phone to use for timings (set to airplane mode to avoid distractions). You might like to use incense if that helps to get you in the right state, but it's not necessary. The simpler we make our space, the better.

HOW YOU MAY FEEL

It's normal to feel a bit crazy and weird when we first practise these principles. These are ancient practices which have been proven to work, but you'll see that they're explained in a way that actually benefits us in our daily lives. Initially you might resist and dismiss their power, but the bottom line is when we passionately apply them, they work. Your life will change in the most amazing ways: situations turn around that have been stuck; relationships are transformed, anxiety, fear and depression are lifted; we feel more joy and happiness; love, self-acceptance and belief in ourselves increases; we come to know our power and potential; and our purpose becomes clear. Doors begin to open, success comes our way and opportunities appear. And all of this happens because we're working from the inside out.

The Experience has the potential to change everything, so if we can get over the awkwardness, in time we won't even care if people laugh at us or judge us, because we'll be too peaceful, happy and sure of ourselves to worry about it.

UNDERSTANDING RESISTANCE

The doubting voice inside our minds might start screaming and shouting at us, listing endless reasons why this is a waste of time and we're too busy. That voice tells us all the reasons we shouldn't start just yet and convinces us it's too difficult or we don't have time to fit it into our daily lives, but it's just a trap.

Our ego tempts us to maintain the status quo. It convinces us we don't need to change and we don't have enough power to change. It's all resistance and actually that's a good sign, because once we're aware of it we know we're just holding ourselves back. And we don't want to do that for any longer than we already have.

THE **DAILY** EXPERIENCE

This isn't mandatory, there's no rule book to say when we do these exercises or for how long. It's the intention we bring to whatever we're doing that matters most. I've tried various routines and this is the best toolbox I've found. If it resonates with you then try it, or adapt as you feel necessary. All I'd say is make sure it's not your smaller self stopping you from doing the work, should you choose to skip some or avoid others altogether.

WHY DO WE DO THIS EVERY DAY?

Most of us spend 99% of our time reading the <u>theory</u> and only put 1% effort into actually <u>practising</u> what we've learnt. The Experience takes us from knowing the theory to experiencing it every day, so that it becomes our way of life. It's one thing to know the principle of forgiveness, but it's an entirely different thing to apply it when we feel someone's taking us for a ride. It's one thing to know about the principle of surrender and letting go, but it's an entirely different thing to apply it when we're not getting what we want and we feel like we're falling behind. It's one thing to know that love is all there is, and another thing to believe in it in the midst of our heartbreak. It takes a strength of mind we don't always know we have to believe in abundance when we have a multitude of bills to pay.

That's why we do this work every day because it's like a daily clear out and the more we do it, the better life gets. It trains our minds against the psychological and attitudinal gravity we experience daily. It places us in a renewed state each morning. It doesn't always guarantee we won't lose it, but at least the times we do will be greatly reduced.

1. **BODY** WORK

THE EXPERIENCE

***

1. SIMPLE BREATHING EXERCISE:

At regular intervals throughout the day, consciously breathe in and out in a steady rhythm.

Inhale energy / Exhale and release

Complete 10 rounds

Remember, it's the quality of your exhale that tells your body you're safe and that everything's ok, which is why it's good to extend the length of the exhale. And it's the quality of your inhale, feeling your tummy expand which brings more air to every cell and organ in your body. You can practise this exercise whilst you're having a break, making a cup of tea, or sat at your desk – you don't have to set aside a specific time. It's helpful to do it at the start of the day, but if you spend the rest of the day stressed and busy then it'll have little impact, so it's massively beneficial to set a regular reminder on your phone to act as a prompt. When you hear that alarm going off, simply complete 10 rounds of optimal breathing.

Notice how this impacts your body, your energy and your mood. If you've been having digestion problems, it'll help to heal that. If you've been having irregular periods, it'll start to bring them back into balance. If you've been depressed, it'll help to lift you out of the darkness. To keep your breathing rhythmical, it's helpful to download a metronome app and set it to 60 beats a second. That way you won't be tempted to rush the exercise.

2. BODY BALANCING EXERCISE:

If you feel you want to try a specific Pranayama technique, you can begin with Nadi Shodhana, otherwise known as

Alternate Nostril Breathing. This exercise balances the energy within our body and removes any blockages.

With your right hand you'll be using your thumb to open and close your right nostril, while your little finger and ring finger will open and close the left nostril.

Breathe in and out a few times through both nostrils to prepare.

1. Using your thumb, close your right nostril and inhale through the left nostril.
2. Now using your two fingers, close the left nostril and release the thumb and exhale through the right nostril.
3. With left nostril still closed, inhale through the right nostril.
4. Using your thumb, close the right nostril, release the two fingers and exhale through the left nostril.

This completes one round. Repeat steps 1 - 4, 10 times. Inhale for 4 counts and exhale for 4 counts, or begin to use the 1:2 ratio and inhale for 4 counts and exhale for 8 counts. (More advanced Pranayamas should be learnt with a qualified teacher. Always seek medical advice before starting any new exercise routines).

3. RELEASE:

At various intervals throughout the day, become aware of the tension in your body and let it all go, especially any tension in your stomach, between your eyes, or in your jaw. Let all that tension melt away.

Say: "I release and let go. I let go of all tension, I let go of all fear, I let go of all guilt, I let go of all pain. I let go and I am free. It is safe to let go. I am free, I am love.

2. **MIND** WORK

THE EXPERIENCE

***

1. PREPARE:

Sit on a meditation cushion (or any cushion or pillow) or on a chair. Try to position your hips slightly higher than your knees. Imagine a piece of string is attached to the crown of your head and is gently encouraging you to sit confidently and upright. Feel the weight of your bottom on the cushion. Drop your chin slightly, relax your shoulders down your back, and close your eyes. Place your hands on your knees, palms either facing upright (signifying being open and receptive) or downwards (signifying surrender and going within). Smile gently to release the tension in your jaw, forehead and behind the eyes. Let your stomach, hips and bottom relax.

Close your eyes and focus on the space between your eyebrows. If your eyes lose focus (which they will), just return them back between your brows. Gradually your breathing will settle and your nervous system will relax. When thoughts arise, keep aiming to go deeper and deeper, seeking to reach the very core of your mind. Sink down below any mental chatter, noise and distractions. If you feel any pain, itches or restlessness, try to focus on reaching further inwards instead. If you desperately need to move, do it gently and with awareness to maintain your sense of stillness.

2. PRACTICE:

Some meditations ask you to stare at a wall or at an object, which personally didn't work for me. Other techniques suggest meditating upon a prayer or an affirmation. Try them all and see which one you connect with most. Transcendental meditation works best for me because it uses a unique short mantra to focus on instead of a long phrase. A mantra means that when your mind wanders you'll be brought back to a focus point. This could be a simple word or phrase that resonates with you, such as 'let go' or 'release'. Some teachers advise you to focus on your breath, but again, this just distracted me. I found that focusing on a simple mantra naturally calmed my breath anyway and kept me in the present moment.

Eventually we'll aim for 20 minutes, but let's start with 10. It's much better to do 10 minutes consistently than 20 minutes once a week. When you reach the point where it becomes uncomfortable, continue for another two minutes and you'll move past the distractions into a deeper sense of peace. If you don't, simply come out of meditation and try again later. There should be no force, no beating yourself up, or judgement about how many thoughts you notice or how uncomfortable you might be. Just keep sinking down within your mind. And always keep your eyes focused between your brows as this helps to still the mind.

3. PEACE:

In time, you'll experience a 'switch click' or a moment when your thoughts temporarily stop and your breathing settles. This switch clicking is similar to turning a computer off and noticing the buzzing of the hard drive stop. Eventually, you'll find yourself looking forward to your meditation practice.

With practice, it's possible to experience a deep and profound sense of peace that's almost hard to explain and the benefits are too vast for me to even try and fit into one chapter. You'll access the place within you where you'll experience perfect peace. You'll achieve a mindset of love and receive all of the strength you need. You'll reach a place where everything becomes possible. And you'll give yourself an opportunity to connect to the wisdom within you every day and to hear its guidance.

Meditation offers you all this and more. And the best thing is it's free and you can do it wherever you go!

I encourage you to practise meditation twice a day. Maybe you could do it once in the morning and once in the evening, or once in the morning and once at lunchtime, or when you get home from work. Find what works for you and stick to it. Even if you don't start with twice a day, just start. Try it. But always do it daily. Maybe start with 10 minutes and, when you feel ready, work up to 20 minutes. Or why not set yourself a 10-day meditation challenge to get you started: 10 minutes of meditation for 10 days. And make a note of the differences you feel, how you start to act instead of react.

4. AFFIRMATIONS:

There are a million affirmations to choose from and they *do* work, but here's the caveat: **only** if they are done consistently for a long enough period **and** if they're felt in every cell in our body. We tend to pick a few, say them for day or a week, and then forget them because we don't see the results as quickly as we'd like. So what do we do if the results don't appear - keep doing them for months at a time, even commit to a few key ones for a year. It takes time and patience to overwrite our thoughts pattens and beliefs, it's not impossible but it doesn't require consistent effort.

3. **HEART** WORK

THE EXPERIENCE

***

Most of us have a backlog of forgiveness work to do but it doesn't have to be a hard task to do. All we need to do is make a start.

STEP 1:
IDENTIFY WHO/WHAT YOU NEED TO FORGIVE

Ask within:

Who or what do I need to forgive?

Who or what do I need to release?

Our conscious mind normally tells us who we *think* we should forgive, but this exercise encourages us to ask at a deeper level and allow our subconscious and superconscious mind to lead us. Sometimes the people or situations that come to mind may surprise us. Sometimes nothing comes to us at all, then   suddenly later on or the next day, someone or something grabs our attention. Sometimes the people or things we need to forgive come to us in our dreams. Once we've asked, this is the time to be aware and notice what comes to mind.

STEP 2:
BLAST GOOD VIBES INSTEAD

Now see these people/situations before you and see the good in them instead. Blast them with good vibes and with love. Wish good fortune for them. See a clear water flowing over them and washing them clean, especially washing over their feet. If it's a situation, see the highest good unfold for everyone concerned. If it's a person, wish them everything you want for yourself. This takes effort, because we get more satisfaction from sending them less than sending the best. Ultimately by doing this, both parties find release, our hearts are healed and opened, and our lives are transformed. And once we experience this feeling we only want more of it. It can help to make a forgiveness list and write everyone and everything down. This acts as a physical, mental, emotional and spiritual clearing.

Instead of holding a grudge, we could feel and say the following repeatedly until we feel a sense of release:

For others:	"I love you … and I forgive you, and I release you to your highest good."
For ourselves:	"I love and forgive myself and I am free."

STEP 3:
RECEIVE MIRACLES

Once you begin to practise forgiveness regularly and let go of all the baggage, you can look forward to all the miracles you'll receive instead. It's often mind blowing what can happen we when we do this work.

And once we do this work consistently, our spirit is transformed, our mindset work becomes easier and more transformational and our bodies let go of the weight we've been carrying around with us. Take a big deep breath and exhale... you've just let go of years of mental and emotional baggage!

4. **SPIRIT** WORK

THE EXPERIENCE

***

STEP 1:
PRAYER

Pray every day, one simple, direct, heartfelt prayer. It doesn't even need to take a minute if it's felt deeply and sincerely enough.

This sounds weird but get down on your knees and join your hands

Pray out loud or silently

Direct your prayers and questions within yourself

See your prayer in your mind, feel it in your heart, and see it extend out into the world

STEP 2:
RECEIVE WISDOM AND GUIDANCE

Before we do anything, we should always ask if it's the right thing to do. No matter how big or small the request is - whether it's asking which route to take or which house to buy - we should always ask for help and guidance before we make any decision. Ask, know you'll be answered, and then wait patiently for the answer. It may not arrive immediately, but it'll come.

Make it a habit that before you make any decision, you ask for guidance first and wait for the answer. It's so easy to want the answer within minutes, but sometimes we have to wait for a reason. From experience, sometimes asking and waiting for an answer has saved me a fortune financially and emotionally.

5. **SOUL** WORK

THE EXPERIENCE

***

VISUALISATION:

I could talk for hours about the power of visualisation, but it's the experience we're after. We all visualise, whether we know it or not, so we may as well make it productive. Our mind doesn't know whether what we're imagining is real, so when we visualise a new way of being, our subconscious mind begins to recreate this image in our lives. And now we know we're working with 95% of our brain's capacity, we're creating a powerful force.

FANCY TRYING IT NOW...?

Close your eyes and imagine the feelings you want to experience - freedom, success, passion, focus, purpose, the feeling of being alive and happy and making progress on your goals.

Now focus on who you would have to *be* in order to create this new version of yourself. How would you behave, look, feel, walk and talk? See this new image of yourself and take time to breathe it in. Expand your energy around it and hold it in your consciousness for a few minutes. And do this daily. It's so simple, yet so powerful.

The real secret to visualisation is to FEEL the feeling you want to experience, not the goal you want to have happen. Feel the feeling as if it it's happening NOW.

IN **SUMMARY:**

MORNING

BODY WORK: *Breathing*

Belly breathing for 5 minutes
(Inhale - energy / Exhale - release)

MIND WORK: *Meditation*

Start with 10 minutes and gradually working up to 20 is
amazing

HEART WORK: *Forgiveness*

Concentrate on one person or situation a day
for a minute or so

SPIRIT WORK: *Prayer*

Focus on one prayer or question a day
for a minute or so

SOUL WORK: *Visualisation*

10 minutes or so visualising with intention
Feel the feelings throughout your body

* * *

DAYTIME

BODY WORK: *Breathing*

The Body Workout
It helps to set your phone alarm to go off at regular intervals throughout the day ago remind you to actually breathe!!!
Try 10 deep breathes in and out fully

EVENING

MIND WORK: *Meditation*

(Start with 10 minutes and build up)

* * *

Remember though that this is a tool box, not a box ticking exercise. Every day when you wake up, ask yourself what you need today. Some days you might need to meditate, others you might need to solely work on forgiveness if you've been angered or irritated by someone. Someone days you might need to prayer deeply. It's about the intention and asking yourself what you need in any given moment. Think of it as the most powerful box of tools you've ever had and use them to your advantage.

FINAL THOUGHTS

It took me years to realise that the various philosophies, belief systems and all of the information I was immersing myself in was simply guiding me back to the potential within myself, to the love that I thought had abandoned me and the inner strength I didn't even know I possessed. It was all teaching me that I was already enough, just like everyone else is, even though I felt judged as hell at times and automatically judged people back.

I always thought the answer to my problems would be found somewhere 'out there' in the world. I thought something inside of me needed to be fixed that hadn't been 'built' correctly. I'd often wonder if everyone else was as messed up as I felt at times?

The answer is: Yes. Many people are. Despite appearances or a social media smokescreen.

But it doesn't need to be this way.

And all I can say from my own experience is that the only thing missing is our awareness of the power, potential and love within ourselves and our willingness to do the work to access it on a daily basis. We can be taught it from an institution or from a religion, but really it's all an experience inside of us and comes alive once we can move past all of the crap we've picked up.

Yes, we may have messed up and chosen incorrectly in the past. Yes, we may have been limited in the past but instead of just doing mindset work, I had to go deeper because there were some other parts of me that clearly needed to be worked on first. The mindset work wasn't working on its own, so I had to find another way. And this book is the other way. And it's only when all of these parts are worked on together that things really began to shift. I truly believe if we were all forced to take a mandatory course on "How to Succeed in Life", this is what we should focus on because it completely changes our energy and what we're putting out there.

Our BODY: *Breathing*

Breathing reconnects us back to the present moment. It's only when I finally found a breathing teacher who taught me how to breathe again, that I came out of a constant state of fight or flight. Breathing correctly would stop many addictions. Physical addictions such as sugar, alcohol and drugs. And mental and emotional addictions like codependency, inadequacy, fear and self-doubt. It helps us to let go, reconnect to the natural order and flow of the Universe.

Our MIND: *Meditation*

Meditation takes our consciousness to another level. It goes way past our conscious mind, to our actual mind beyond the fear we've learned. This is where our actual mind lives. This is where we live from a place of power, instead of constant fear.

Our HEART: *Forgiveness*

Forgiveness reminds us of the love within us. We're told to "be kind" but it's hard to do that when we live in a constant state of attack and defence. Always trying to protect ourselves from ever being hurt again. It's not like we need to go out to find or buy more love. Forgiveness just reminds us of the love we already have and lets it flow again.

Our SPIRIT: *Prayer*

Prayer lifts our vibe and takes our thoughts higher. Whenever we're depressed, it's our spirit, our mental attitude which has taken a hit. Prayer can be the last thing we want to do, it can be the last thing we think has any potential to help us. In key moments in my life, I can honestly say it's been the one thing that's saved it.

Our SOUL: Visualisation

Visualisation helps us to connect with our soul and expand it. When we surrender into our greatness instead, and stop resisting it. Our purpose starts to become crystal clear and when we're living our purpose, we're automatically less likely to dip back into depression. Our soul begins to come alive again when we're not fighting life anymore. When we're willing, however reluctantly, to grow into the person we know we can be.

The combination of these practices allows us to effect a powerful change in our lives. From the inside-out. Now all parts of our psyche are aligned, we become unstoppable. It's not to say we'll never dip again, but the dips won't be so brutal and the rebound will be quicker. This is where some people think life will become boring, but this is where our life begins to take off.

One of my favourite lines from *A Course In Miracles* is: **"Remember, you will have to go through the clouds before you can reach the light."** You might feel like you're in the clouds right now and that there's a lot of them to work through. But it's not a bad thing and it doesn't mean anything is wrong. The experience that lies beyond the doubt and fear is so worth the effort.

Right now more than ever, the World needs your gifts, your talents and your power. It's all inside of you. It's time to reconnect and let it out. Every.Single.Day.

Love,

Laura-Jane x

ABOUT THE AUTHOR

Hi, I'm Laura-Jane,

The former Queen of Inadequacy and Self-Doubt!

A woman who spent tens of thousands of pounds seeking out the best gurus and teachers, and travelling the world to find 'the answer' to years of questioning what was wrong and what was missing, whilst creating a little bit of chaos along the way.

I'm a **coach** specialising in **Intimate Relationships**, which always start with the relationship we have with ourselves. I'm also the host of **The Rise-Higher Podcast**, and a student of *A Course In Miracles*. My focus is on creating change from the Inside-Out.

Please don't hesitate to reach out.

I'd **love** to hear from you.

Email: **laurajanehand8@gmail.com**
Website: **www.laurajanehand.com**

Instagram: @**laurajanehand**
Linked In: **linkedin.com/in/laurajanehand**
Podcast link: **wavve.link/laurajanehand**

Disclaimer

This book is designed to provide information and motivation to the readers. The work is the sole expression and opinion of the author. It is sold with the understanding that the author is not engaged to render any type of psychological, medical, or any other kind of professional advice. Please seek a qualified teacher on a personal basis for further information. The information provided in this book is designed to provide helpful information on the subjects discussed. No guarantees are provided. This book is not meant to be used, nor should it be used, to diagnose or treat any medical condition.

For diagnosis or treatment of any medical problem, consult your own physician. Please seek medical advice before carrying out any of the exercises in this book. The publisher and author are not responsible for any specific health needs that may require medical supervision and are not liable for any damages or negative consequences from any action, application or preparation, to any person reading or following the information in this book. Neither the publisher nor author shall be liable for any physical, psychological, emotional, financial, or commercial damages, including, but not limited to, special, incidental, consequential or other damages.

You are responsible for your own choices, actions, and results. References are provided for informational purposes only and all names have been changed. Although the author and publisher have made every effort to ensure that the information in this book was correct at press time, the author and publisher do not assume and hereby disclaim any liability to any party for any loss, damage, or disruption caused by errors or omissions, whether such errors or omissions result from negligence, accident, or any other cause.

Printed in Great Britain
by Amazon